Good Old Days Remembers the *Little Country* SCHOOLHOUSE

Edited by Ken and Janice Tate

HOUSE of
WHITE
BIRCHES

PUBLISHERS
SINCE 1947

Editors: Ken and Janice Tate
Associate Editor: Barb Sprunger
Copy Editors: Läna Schurb, Mary Nowak

Production Coordinator: Brenda Gallmeyer
Design/Production Artist: Beverly Jenkins
Traffic Coordinator: Sandra Beres
Production Assistants: Carol Dailey, Chad Tate

Photography: Tammy Christian, Jeff Chilcote, Jennifer Fourman
Photography Assistant: Linda Quinlan
Photography Stylist: Arlou Wittwer

Publishers: Carl H. Muselman, Arthur K. Muselman
Chief Executive Officer: John Robinson
Marketing Director: Scott Moss
Product Development Director: Vivian Rothe
Publishing Services Manager: Brenda Wendling

Printed in the United States of America
First Printing: 1999
Library of Congress Number: 99-073201
ISBN: 1-882138-50-3

Every effort has been made to ensure the accuracy of the material
in this book. However, the publisher is not responsible for research
errors or typographical mistakes in this publication.

We would like to thank the following for the art prints used in this book:
Mill Pond Press: "Just Before the Bell" by Jim Daly, page 20; "A Gift of Time" by Jim Daly, page 44.
Both by arrangement with Mill Pond Press Inc.
For information on art prints, contact Mill Pond Press, Venice, FL 34292, (800) 535-0331.
Wild Wings Inc.: "Country School" by Lee Stroncek, page 28. By arrangement with
Wild Wings Inc., Lake City, MN 55042, (800) 445-4833.
We would also like extend a very special thank-you to Shirley Steele, Washington, Iowa, and Wynne Steele,
Riverside, Iowa, for the use of their historical school-day treasures on pages 35, 45, 63, 129, 135, 139 and 153.

Dear Friends of the Good Old Days,

Like most of you, some of my fondest memories of childhood revolve around the years I spent in school.

My "larnin'" days were spent in little country schoolhouses in the hills of the Ozark Mountains. There, I picked up the three R's and a whole lot more.

I learned you had to keep your feet in your shoes, even on late summer days when your toes were so hot you thought they would burst into flames—and on warm spring days when fresh, green grass beckoned bare feet.

I learned a bit about love. Wilma Hensley was my first school days crush. She was from the small community just down the road from our farm. In the second grade, I endured other boys' hoots and derision, and gave Wilma a couple of Mama's fresh oatmeal cookies. We ate them at lunch with a glass of milk on the steps of the little stone schoolhouse.

And there was so much more. I learned about hard work from helping Teacher with schoolhouse chores, like cleaning the blackboard and carrying water. I learned about love of country from reciting the Pledge of Allegiance each morning. I learned about faith, hope and charity through morning devotionals before school prayer was found to be unconstitutional. I guess I learned pretty much everything I needed—and all of that without the aid of television, computers and the rest of education's modern trappings.

I hope you enjoy this collection of school days stories. They remember the best of the days when the one-room school reigned supreme. They will conjure up a lot of memories of the little country schoolhouses back in the Good Old Days.

Sincerely,

Ken Tate

Contents

Yuletides, Halloweens and Other Special Days • 87

Schoolrooms & School Yards • 129

"A Ragged Beggar Sleeping"

Chapter One

B ack in the days of my primary education, there was no kindergarten, head start or preschool. Children went to school at age 6 and that was to first grade. Many times first grade was in the same room with several other grades, but the interaction with older children was usually a positive experience for the younger of us.

Since I have a Columbus Day birthday, Mama and Daddy decided I should start school before I turned 6. I had watched with thinly veiled envy while older brother Dennis attended school alone.

But now it was my turn, so on that warm, early September morning I checked and double-checked my satchel to make sure I had all of the necessities of a mature first-grader—No. 2 pencil, writing tablet, lunch packed in a paper bag—and then headed out into the world of education.

One of my favorite poems by John Greenleaf Whittier is "In School-Days." In it he speaks of the little country schoolhouse: "Still sits the school-house by the road, A ragged beggar sleeping; And it still the sumachs grow, and blackberry vines are creeping." The school of my youth was not exactly "a ragged beggar sleeping," but by the time I passed through its hallowed doors, it had already seen its better days. A stone edifice—stones were easy to come by in those rocky Ozark Mountains, I suppose—it stood at the top of a tall hill. It was the same school my mother had attended, so the masons' work had expertly stood the test of time.

From the letters and articles I have received over the years as editor of *Good Old Days* magazine, many of my readers have an extraordinary memory of their first day in school. I do not. I know we sat quietly and obediently, following the directions of Miz Leatherman (I remember her name), but particulars escape me. All particulars but one, I'm embarrassed to admit.

Sometime in mid-morning we were released for recess, as I'm sure most primary schools did. And, also like most of the small country schools at that time, our "playground"—a converted field, really—was equipped only with a couple of swings from tree limbs and a crude baseball field.

Still, recess was something I could do well! My toes ached to be out of those confounded shoes, and in the warmth of the late summer sun I shucked them faster than an ear of corn. For the next 10 minutes or more I was in heaven. I ran with friends, threw rocks, harassed girls—all of the fun things a first-grader loves to do. Dennis never once acted as if he were any relation to me at all—but that was fine with me. Who needed a mentor now? I was in my element at recess.

I followed a lizard down a slope to a small rock bluff. By the time I realized I wasn't going to be able to catch him and returned to the playground, all of my mates had mysteriously disappeared. What the heck! I had played alone before, and I knew they would all be back sooner or later.

After a few minutes, I looked up from the dirt pile I was playing in to see Miz Leatherman approaching with a rather stern look on her face. After a brief discussion about truancy I was escorted by the ear back into the little country schoolhouse and my first taste of education in the Good Old Days.
—*Ken Tate*

The Pioneer Schoolhouse

By Ben Thorman

The Cantwell School, in 1912, was a little one-room schoolhouse only 4½ miles from our ranch in the Osage Hills north of Kaw City, Okla. The road, like all other roads in the country, had no paving, no blacktop and not even any gravel. There were no bridges across small streams, and in case of a hard rain, the water would get a little high for the wagons and buggies, but we could always get across on horseback. The higher the water, the more fun it was to cross. It was dusty or muddy all the time; however, because of such little travel grass covered all of the road except the main trails and ruts.

In case of a cold, blowing snowstorm, the hour it took to get to school or church proved to be a mighty cold experience. If we were going in the old buggy or surrey, we would put a lantern or some heated stones by our feet under the lap robe. A lap robe in those days was a well-known and very necessary piece of equipment in winter. It was used in the buggy and surrey just as regularly as the cowboy used the saddle blanket.

Our teacher, Miss Hines, taught all grades, one through eight. Each grade would be called to the front of the room as it came their turn to explain their lesson and get the assignment for the next day. Order was reasonably good in this crowded room; no one was allowed to talk or even whisper unless they were given permission from the teacher after raising their hand.

Our teacher was so nice and we all wanted to please her to the extent that discipline was normally no problem.

There were no spoiled children in this school, if we judged by the old saying "Spare the rod and spoil the child." If a child needed correcting, there was no dean of boys or girls, nor a principal's office to send them to. One might just be called to the front of the room for a good paddling right in front of everyone. Sometimes the punishment might be to stay in during recess or after school, but the worst and most humiliating thing was to have to stand in the corner. However, our teacher was so nice and we all wanted to please her to the extent that discipline was normally no problem.

If a boy or girl signaled with one or two fingers, he or she would get permission to leave the room and go to the old outhouse which answered the purpose of a rest room. There were two of these old outhouses, one on each side back corner of the school grounds, one marked "Boys" and the other "Girls." There were heavy wooden latches on the door, one on the outside and one on the inside. If the door was unlatched from the outside, it was considered to be in use and you had to wait your turn. In each outhouse was an old Sears and Roebuck or Montgomery Ward catalog. Throwing rocks against the little buildings, just to scare some pretty girl or little boy, was strictly forbidden. However, accidents would sometimes happen.

There was a barn by the school because most of the children rode horseback. A big, old wood stove stood in the center of the room, and we older boys kept the fire going all day. There was a well for our drinking water and everyone brought their lunch of corn bread, homemade sausage, smokehouse ham, wild rabbit and duck, potatoes, homemade bread and home-canned jelly, or perhaps an onion and an apple.

The main reason we children loved going to school was the joy of recess time. When the little bell was tapped, we all had to file out by classes and in order, but as soon as the door was cleared, the noise and fun began. The boys would play mumbletypeg, and wrestle and scuffle around while the little girls would jump rope, play jacks, or just run and play. We would all choose up sides in such games as Blackman, Steal the Bacon, Hopscotch, Red Rover or The Flying Dutchman.

On Sunday, the little building became our church. It was pretty crowded for the Sunday school classes. It took an active girl to play the organ, because it had to be pumped with both feet for the air supply. Everyone joined in singing the old hymns: *Rock of Ages, Jesus is Calling, Jesus Saves, When the Role is Called Up Yonder, The Old Rugged Cross, Sweet Hour of Prayer, Softly and Tenderly* and a few others.

Each spring there would be an old-fashioned revival which would end on Sunday with a special day that would include a dinner-on-the-ground and preaching all day. No family would go home alone after church on Sunday; two or three families would go to one of the ranches for a big meal and a good visit.

Christmas-time at this pioneer school was something never to be forgotten. A big Christmas tree from one of the neighboring ranches was decorated with cranberries and popcorn strung on long threads, popcorn balls, and chains made of colorful paper links, each cut and pasted by hand. There was a present and a small sack of candy for each child. The candy was all homemade, and there might be a few home-roasted peanuts in the sack.

There were no electric lights in this little building and we didn't even have Coleman lanterns. We used the old-fashioned coal-oil lamps with the little felt wick that had to be trimmed once in a while. We also used some candles, mostly homemade.

Almost every child had some little part in the Christmas play and some man would bring the big surprise by acting as Santa Claus. The evening would always end with the real story of Christmas.

These were the experiences that made the Good Old Days in that pioneer school so special.❖

In School-Days

Still sits the school-house by the road,
A ragged beggar sleeping;
And it still the sumachs grow,
And blackberry vines are creeping.

Within, the master's desk is seen,
Deep scarred by raps official;
The warping floor, the battered seats,
The jack-knife's carved initial;

The charcoal frescoes on its wall;
Its door's worn sill, betraying
The feet that, creeping slow to school,
Went storming out to playing!

Long years ago a winter sun
Shown over it at setting;
Lit up its western windowpanes,
And low eaves' icy fretting.

It touched the tangled golden curls
And brown eyes full of grieving,
Of one who still her steps delayed
When all the school were leaving.

For near her stood the little boy
Her childish favor singled:
His cap pulled low upon a face
Where pride and shame were mingled.

Pushing with restless feet the snow
To right and left, he lingered: —
As restlessly her tiny hands
The blue-checked apron fingered.

He saw her lift her eyes; he felt
The soft hand's light caressing.
And heard the tremble of her voice,
As if a fault confessing.

"I'm sorry that I spelt the word:
I hate to go above you,
Because,"—the brown eyes
lower fell,—
"Because you see, I love you!"

Still memory to a gray-haired man
that sweet child-face is showing.
Dear girl! the grasses on her grave
Have 40 years been growing!

He lives to learn, in life's hard school,
How few who pass above him
Lament their triumph and his loss,
Like her,—because they love him.

— By John Greenleaf Whitter (1870)

Little White Schoolhouse

By Lucille Howe

Much has been written about country schools. I will try not to repeat memories others have reported. I have special ones of my own.

Did your school board visit school on opening day? Ours did. When we arrived at the school yard on that exciting first day, we would find two teams of horses hitched to spring wagons, and tied to the big metal ring on the south side of the building. One team belonged to Mr. Abel, a plump, full-bearded, jolly man with a German accent. The other driver was Mr. Somers, a small, goateed man of English descent. The third board member was Mr. Erickson, who always walked across fields to the school yard. We children were all a bit in awe of him because he had only one eye.

When we took our lunch pails into the schoolroom, we would see the three men and the teacher in conversation. Later, when we were summoned from play, the three men would be seated in the back of the room on the only three chairs we had. I have sometimes wondered if they were the reason we had just three. Sometime during the first hour or so, the visitors would quietly leave.

At the time, this all seemed very normal, but when I became a teacher, I thought back with great sympathy for the young woman trying to get her classes organized under the scrutiny of three perhaps totally strange men, if she was new at the school. The board members would probably visit again sometime during the term, but not necessarily together.

We had neither piano nor organ, and no songbooks, yet we sang and enjoyed it nearly every morning for opening exercises.

Visiting parents were rare except on special occasions, but the county superintendent came at least twice a year. During my first few years in school, the superintendents were men; then a woman, Miss Madson, was elected. She would come in a one-seated buggy, driving a single horse, and unannounced. However, by the time she got her horse tied up, we pupils and the teacher were usually forewarned. Someone near a window would spot and recognize her buggy, and whispers and gestures would alert us. When Miss Madson came in without knocking, we were all on good behavior.

We had neither piano nor organ, and no songbooks, yet we sang and enjoyed it nearly every morning for opening exercises. To teach us a new song, the teacher would write the words on the blackboard. We

who were old enough were expected to copy them in what we called our copy books. One morning the teacher would stand up in front of us and sing a verse. Next she would sing a line at a time, and we would sing it after her. In later years, I found out that we were not always singing exactly the notes the composer intended, but the young ladies did their best.

At least one teacher used to write what she called "mottoes" on the board for us to copy and memorize. Some examples are: "Honesty is the best policy", "All that glitters is not gold" and "Time and tide wait for no man." I think she expected these sayings to build character in us. After we'd supposedly learned a few dozen of these, we'd have a

Friday afternoons! How we looked forward to them! What we did depended on the teacher.

"motto-down"—like a spell-down, only we didn't choose sides. It was every child for himself and the one who could keep on remembering mottoes the longest was the winner.

We had real spell-downs, too, and a couple of times a year, a question box. The box was usually the wooden box with a sliding cover in which the school purchased chalk, probably 100 nice, long pieces to a box. (Remember how wonderful it was to get a new, long piece to write with? And how soon it became two or more short ones?)

For a day or so, we were encouraged to write questions on small slips of paper and put them in the box. Each question was directed to a certain pupil by name. Presumably the questions were related to our studies, but a few jokes always found their way into the box. For instance, the day a boy and girl went through the ice while skating on the creek at noon, they were asked such questions as, "Were you scared? Are you dry yet? Didn't you hear the ice cracking?"

On Friday afternoon, someone was appointed to read the questions to the pupils who answered as best they could.

Ah! Friday afternoons! How we looked forward to them! What we did depended on the teacher. One was strong for watercolor painting. We painted pictures of many kinds of birds one year for our Liberty Bell Bird Club notebooks. Another time we did calendars. Another teacher had us do a lot of raffia work. An artistically inclined young woman would have us doing freehand drawing and cutting.

Before Christmas we made simple gifts for our parents. For Valentine's Day—ah, Valentine's Day!—we had another box, and for weeks we made valentines. At school we got some construction paper for those we made on Friday afternoon; for the rest, we had to use our tablet paper. I'm sure there were parental complaints about that time of year, when children announced they needed new tablets. At home, we were lucky if there was a

The little country schoolhouse
Of which so many write
Was always painted red, it seems,
But mine was painted white.

There's where I learned the three big Rs,
Plus several Ps and Qs,
And miscellaneous other things
That in my life I'd use.

That tiny, old, white schoolhouse
Was replaced by another;
That one, though new and larger,
Was white, like the other.

Then I started teaching school,
And, as you may have guessed,
The buildings that I taught in
Were white, just like the rest.

So, sing of your little red schoolhouse,
And of your mem'ries write:
Someday I'll write a tribute
To the schoolhouse that was white.

wallpaper catalog we could use; otherwise, it was probably brown wrapping paper.

Remember collapsible drinking cups? When I started school in 1906, we all drank out of the same dipper from an open pail—if we were lucky enough to *have* water. There was no well on the school grounds. Two older pupils would carry a pail between them from the nearest farm, almost a quarter of a mile away. This was usually done at noon. There would be perhaps 20 thirsty children waiting for a drink after eating a dry lunch. By afternoon recess, one might well find the pail empty. Many cold or stormy days we had nothing to drink all day, unless we brought it from home, and few of us did that. Then a new law was passed, requiring schools to provide a more sanitary way of dispensing water. We had a crock with a faucet on it, and each pupil had to provide his own cup. Tin cups, cracked cups, old cups, new cups appeared. Then one day, one lucky kid came with a collapsible aluminum cup. How we envied that youngster! After a year or so of begging, hinting and hoping, most of us had those wonderful cups, which were no more sanitary than the old ones but took up less space in our desks.

Most of us had slates in my early years. A few years later, when I taught, there were no slates in the room, for which I was duly grateful. There can be no more devastating noise in a fairly quiet room than the screech of a mishandled slate pencil, and a slate falling on the floor will turn all heads.

Only one thing competed with slates in noisy falls—pencil boxes. Those wooden boxes with hinged covers flew open, strewing pencils, pen holders, steel pen points, erasers and often a pencil sharpener or penknife. These last were necessary because we had no wall pencil sharpener.

Then there was seat work, something very necessary to keep the small folk busy while the older ones recited. A picture to color might keep a child occupied for five minutes; puzzles didn't take much longer. You see, teachers of those days didn't have beautifully planned workbooks for every class, so they often used the cut-up letters and numbers printed on pieces of cardboard hardly a quarter-inch square. Each child was given a handful of the letters or numbers and was assigned a few sentences or problems to build. This would keep little minds and fingers busy for a long time.

Once a year we'd get a few new books. What a thrill it was to have new books to take home and read!

I confess I used such seat work when I taught little ones, but if I were to teach again, I would never do so. The squares were too small for clumsy young fingers, and the letters too tiny for such young eyes, but that was not the worst of it. About the time a pupil got the assignment all built and was awaiting the teacher's approval, the youngster in the seat ahead of him might jiggle the desk, or swing his elbow back on it. Either way, a half-hour's work could be wiped out in a second.

We had what the teacher called "the chart," a number of big sheets with diagrams and other teaching aids hung on a metal stand. I remember only a few. The first ones were for beginners; we learned our first words and letters from it. The three others I recall were for teaching physiology or health instruction. There was one of the skeleton, naming the bones; one of the circulatory system; and one of the nerves of the whole body.

When I think of the chart, I visualize the teacher pointing to things on it with the pointer. That pointer fascinated me. I loved to watch the teacher use it, loved still more to handle it myself, to "climb a word ladder on the board" or to play school at recess. It was about 3 feet long, tapered, with a rubber tip on the small end and a circle screwed in the large end with which to hang it on a nail.

We had a small library—not a room, just a couple of shelves in an open cupboard. Once a year we'd get a few new books. What a thrill it was to have new books to take home and read! The teacher would probably keep back a book or two to read to us for opening exercises after noon. I remember *Black Beauty, Beautiful Joe and Flipwing, The Spy* being read to us. Among the books we had were *Anne of Green Gables* and some of the other Anne books, *The Five Little Peppers* books and *Dandelion Cottage.*

With regard to textbooks, the first year we had two readers, the dear old *Rose Primer* and *Baldwin's First Reader.* We had the *Baldwin Readers* for all grades, but no supplementary readers, as I remember. When we'd gone through the reader for our grade, we'd go back to the beginning and go over it again.

There were the *Milne Arithmetics, Montgomery History* texts, the *Herrington Speller* and the *Metcalf Grammar.* When I was in the eighth grade, the poor rural teachers with all eight grades were asked to add another subject to the curriculum for the older pupils, namely agriculture. For this, we used a Wilson text.

Early in the year the supplies the teacher had ordered would arrive—construction paper and drawing paper, a big jar of library paste, and a big bottle of ink to fill the little inkwells on the desks. There might be something special like the raffia, but the money allowed for supplies was very limited.

The paste smelled so good that some of the children could not resist eating some. Using it was messier than using the bottled glue children use now. The trouble was, you had to use your fingers to apply it, then use those same small fingers to handle whatever you were pasting. A young first-grade teacher told me she solved that problem by teaching the children from the beginning to use only their pinkies to spread the paste.

Our school was old enough to maintain the tradition of a boys' side of the room and a girls' side. The ones in the little seats in the middle did get mixed up somewhat. The biggest desks were right against the wall on each side, which meant that some were at least partly in front of a window. It was no wonder that in winter, there were usually two or three sitting by the stove, warming their feet. By contrast, the little room was often too hot by afternoon.

That tiny building was ideal for playing one of our favorite games, "Antie-Over." We played a lot of different games, but I don't recall that we ever played baseball or workup as my pupils did in later years. Perhaps no one had a bat or ball to bring to school. We loved it when our teacher would come out and play with us, enjoying games like Farmer in the Dell and Cat and Rat.

We looked forward to spring when we could pick mayflowers in the meadow across the creek. They were really pasqueflowers, but we knew them only as mayflowers.

Then there were the cold days when we had to stay inside. How the teachers ever put up with our games in that little space, I don't know. We played Fruit Basket Upset, Colors and Clap In–Clap Out—all noisy diversions.

In the winter, the noon break was usually shortened to a half-hour, presumably so pupils got home before the chill of evening, or so parents coming for their children could get back earlier for chores.

I always loved school, and very few memories are anything but pleasant when I think back to my eight years in old District 8 and my little white schoolhouse. ❖

The Old School Bell

There's a melody it seems I hear again
through Childhood's ears;
Hear its mellow notes re-echoing
across the passing years,
As Memory reaches back through time
to weave her magic spell,
Bringing back to me the music
of that Old School Bell.

To its call, which then seemed strident,
but which now would sound so sweet,
I reluctantly responded
on my naked, suntanned feet.
In bib overalls and straw hat,
with a book my only load,
I'd go loafing off each morning
down the old dirt road.

Through the warm and drowsy summer,
through the winter's frosty chill,
Came that loud, insistent clamor
(seems like I can hear it still!),
Torn by pangs of mental anguish,
I'd go plodding off once more
On that oft-repeated journey
to that schoolhouse door.

Didn't always have things easy;
sometimes life was sort of hard;
I have often eaten lunches of cold flapjacks
spread with lard,
Still, the way my heart is yearning,
I can find no words to tell,
Just to heed once more the summons
of that Old School Bell!

— By Albert E. Graham

Subscription Schools

By Jeryl A. Watson

What were the schools like in the Indian Territory of Oklahoma prior to statehood? This was the question I asked my dad, who came with his family to live in Indian Territory near Henryetta while he was in his early teens. When Dad arrived in 1903, there was no school for white children in the rural community where he lived. There were boarding schools for Indian boys and girls. These were maintained as mission projects by various religious denominations. The Indian children who lived near my dad attended a boarding school in Wetumka, about 30 miles away.

During the next year the white settlers donated lumber and labor to build a schoolhouse near Salem. It measured about 12 feet by 18 feet, with a cast-iron heater which burned wood. It was furnished with a blackboard and some homemade benches, but no desks. There was a community water bucket with a dipper. The older students took turns carrying water from the well at a log house down the road a piece. The toilets were crude outhouses with open pits and walls made of vertical poles covered with burlap bags.

Since Granddad had done some teaching before leaving Alabama, he was asked to be the teacher. He agreed to do so reluctantly, since he had moved west in hopes of improving his ailing health. But times were hard and he desperately needed the money to support his family.

The school was called a "subscription school." There was no revenue from state or county; in fact, there was no state or county! The parents paid Granddad $1 per month for each child he taught. He had about 20 students, four of which were his own. This sounds like a very low salary, but at that time wages were very low for all types of work.

Granddad and his four youngsters started before daylight and walked the 4 miles to the school building. Upon arrival, they built a fire in the heater, swept the floors and filled the water bucket.

The children's clothing was often patched, but they were clean. The boys wore bib overalls, blue work shirts and long underwear with drop seats. On their heads they wore caps with a bill and earflaps that could be turned down when the weather turned cold. The girls wore long gingham dresses, several petticoats and high-button shoes.

Each student carried his own small slate for working arithmetic and for writing spelling lessons.

There were no pencils or writing paper. Each student carried his own small slate for working arithmetic and for writing spelling lessons. Each student had his own books which he carried home at night for safekeeping.

Granddad and his four children carried their lunch to school in a big bucket. It consisted of hog meat, cornbread, beans, butter and sorghum molasses.

The students devised their own entertainment for recess. The girls brought their dolls and played with them. The boys played "One-Eyed Cat" with a homemade ball, made by unraveling an old sock and winding the yarn around a small rock, and a bat, made by cutting and shaping a young hickory sapling. The boys would often sneak a chew of Erice Greenville chewing tobacco.

Although Granddad did not live to see it, the coming of statehood two years later was to bring many improvements in educational opportunities for children in the new state. ❖

School-Yard Games

By Frances Heaton

The games we played during recess (15 minutes in morning and afternoon) and during the noon hour were probably quite typical of those in other country schools of my era. However, when we tired of the same old thing, the creative pupils from District 13 in western Nebraska sometimes invented original games that were ingenious and at times downright dangerous.

District 13 was also known by the more euphonious name of North Star. It was the typical one-room country school, circa 1911. Lunch pails more often than not were syrup pails. Our double desks with their inkwells were lined up on both sides of the potbellied stove. Rows of hooks at the back of the room held soggy coats and mittens or bonnets and caps, depending on the season.

Crack the Whip is now always played on ice. But we played it as a running game in much the same way, linking hands, running, then the leader stopping suddenly and "cracking off" some of the players.

We were always choosing up sides for something, and as usual, the strongest or most popular players were chosen first.

When the usual games, such as Drop the Handkerchief, Blind Man's Bluff and Beckon, Beckon began to pall—especially for the older kids— it wasn't so hard to invent a new game. While the little kids shouted, "All-ee, all-ee out's in free!" or, "Six and four are 10, chase the red lion (it always came out "line") from his den!" the older boys and girls made up games, some competitive, some just for fun and some rather "far out."

One such game had to do with tumbleweeds. Tumbleweeds in western Nebraska were Russian thistles, pronounced by almost everyone as "Rooshian" thistles. If you called them "Rushin" thistles, you were thought to be putting on airs and were considered snooty. Russian thistles grew where and when nothing else would grow, and often reached huge proportions, sometimes several feet in circumference. Take one such tumbleweed, tie a stout cord or twine to the stem end, have a boy or girl hold the other end of the cord, and add a wind which blew as only it blows in western Nebraska, and down the country road you'd go like a ship in full sail before a stiff breeze.

One of our games was a spin-off of Crack the Whip. First, we chose up sides. (We were always choosing up sides for something, and, as

usual, the strongest or most popular players were chosen first. I was always chosen last; I was the smallest and cried easily.) Then each side formed a chain by holding hands, or made an even stronger link by holding each other's wrists. The leader from one side then selected a strong player who ran at full speed to the other side and attempted to break through the hold of two players. If he succeeded, he could claim the players at the lower end for his side. The same action was then repeated by the other team. The side which had the most players when the bell rang was declared the winner.

Perhaps the game which had the strongest appeal, the game which easily could have broken arms and legs (but miraculously never did), was called simply Jumping Board. So far as I know, it was invented by North Star and was unique to that school. Equipment consisted of a plank just wide enough to stand on with both feet and thick enough to be strong but still have plenty of spring. This was laid across a

One jumped on his end of the board, and the other flew into the air, only to come down on his end.

support which might be pieces of wood piled together, or a log, not too large and anchored firmly. The higher the balance, the more adventurous the sport.

Two pupils teamed up, usually of about the same weight, although the plank could be adjusted to compensate for a difference. The partners took their places at each end of the plank. One jumped on his end of the board, and the other flew into the air, only to come down with considerable force on his end, sending his partner zooming up into the air. Some of the stronger and more agile boys and girls became so adept that they were flying into the air so high that they could see over the schoolhouse.

Games played on the modern school ground, with its well-surfaced play area and sophisticated equipment, may be better organized, more closely supervised and perhaps just as competitive. But I'm sure none are more fun and certainly not as original as those played at North Star, District 13. ❖

Washing Dishes

By Audrey Carli

As I've gotten older, I've viewed stacks of dirty dishes with the feeling, *Go away, please.* But they've never left on their own. Thousands of dishes have swished through my sink in my lifetime—as they have gone through most housewives' sudsy water. Only when I was a child was I almost breathless in my hope that the teacher would choose me and another classmate to wash at least 25 cups and a huge, enameled coffee pot which had held the steaming cocoa our class had consumed after recess.

During the Depression, at recess time the young women who worked for the N.Y.A. often helped teacher with errands: cooking prunes, brewing cocoa, slicing and sectioning grapefruit, or preparing some other surplus food commodity for grade-school children. But after the treats had been enjoyed, two pupils were selected to wash the dishes.

How we yearned to be the chosen few! But there was a catch: All our schoolwork had to be finished and done carefully. Now do you see why many of us worked so hard to do our best on our classroom assignments? There was always that underlying motive: *Hurry and finish without mistakes, if possible, in case there's a treat and dishes need washing.* A few of us knew this secret and kept it well, and managed to be chosen a few times each year to wash and dry that heap of dishes.

Some days, the minutes after recess found us sitting at our desks with steaming cups of cocoa, or sauce dishes filled with wrinkly, shiny brown prunes in dark sauce, or pinkish-yellow grapefruit with bittersweet juice and pulp that made your mouth water just looking at it. After the last spoon stopped clicking, the dishes were gathered and the teacher selected the dishwashers. We sat, breathless, until the names were called. I'll never forget my turns.

The helper and I walked through the silent hallway to another classroom that had a closet and a deep, white sink. I never quite got over how quiet a hall could get after hundreds of feet had filed through it only minutes before.

When we started sudsing the dishes with the steaming water gurgling from the tap, we quietly discussed how lucky we were to have gotten out of math or whichever class we happened to have missed! Then, after the last spoon was dried, we hung the long, rough white towel on the wire line near the sink and returned to the classroom to find two dozen heads bent over desks. We slipped back into our routine, hands wrinkled, but our spirits smooth.

To this day, whenever I am confronted with spaghetti-stained plates or gravy-splattered bowls or cups stained with dried-on chocolate, I begin to get that hemmed-in feeling. But a recollection of the days when dishwashing was fun lifts my mood at once, and I tackle the dirty dishes with a fresh mood as the suds cover the same hands that liked being in dishwater years ago during grade-school days.

By the time flashes of memories flick through my mind, the dishes are clean, drying sparkly in the drainer. No longer are dishes a burden—all because of the nostalgia formed with recess treats back in the Depression. ❖

> *We quietly discussed how lucky we were to have gotten out of math or whichever class we happened to have missed!*

Baucom vs. Goose Creek

By B. Ferne Hunter

*G*oose Creek School always challenged Baucom to a spelling match sometime during the school year, and the match was the talk of Baucom for weeks before and after the event.

Those were the days in which learning was for the sake of learning, and much store was set by the ability to spell long and catchy words, such as "phthisis," "pneumonia" and "souvenir." If one knew that there were two Ts and one I in "battalion," that "medallion" contained one D and two Ls, and that "committee" was doubled up all the way through with two Ms and two Ts and two Es, he had ranking at Baucom School.

Also, those were the days when there was lots of time and favorable conditions for long thoughts. The days were long—ah! much longer than they are now—and there was bliss and contentment even in the discordant rasp of the jar fly's song in the hickory tree by the window, for it was a part of the lull of a long, dreamy afternoon at Baucom.

The spelling match took place only once a year, and since it was an affair wrought with no small amount of hard work in preparation, few ever missed it.

Sitting by the back window, as Iva and I did, we could cast dreamy eyes at the blue of the distant horizon toward the peaceful Pine Dale woods and fix in mind the word "battalion," remembering the two Ts as in "battle," without actually connecting the word to a gory incident such as the invasion of Normandy, which was much too real in 1944. Yes, those were the days of long, long leisurely thoughts.

As the long fingers of the afternoon shadows of the great hickory trees enveloped the old gray buildings, we knew that the time for spelling was rolling around. It was in all seriousness that we, the "A" spelling class, took the floor and spelled "chagrin," "unquestionably," "noncommunicativeness" and "honisoitquimalypense," and neither Iva, Verla, Willie, Wilbur, Berlin, Callie nor I missed a word.

Recitations by the spelling classes climaxed the day. Another day at Baucom School had passed into oblivion. Who cared if the pink ginghams, fresh in the morning, were wilted now from perspiration, and if there was a 2-mile walk home under the August sun and chores to do after that? Hadn't we experienced a glorious day, meeting with the boys and girls, learning new things, and anticipating a spelling match?

And so August passed into September, and September was in its very last days. The clear air had a tinge of autumn in it. The masses of goldenrod growing on the side of Carpenter Hill had been too tempting for us, and we had picked great armfuls of it that morning on our way to school.

We stood to sing *The Schoolhouse on the Hill*. I never shall forget how the little one-room school looked, bedecked with goldenrod in stone jars, the golden sunshine, crisp with autumn, making a great shaft through the east door and reaching almost to the recitation benches in the front of the room. Then it happened. A messenger from Goose Creek School appeared in the long shaft of sunshine, bringing us the challenge we had expected and which we accepted with loud, long applause.

We could scarcely wait for Saturday night to come. That was the time set for the match. There were many preparations to make before the 10-mile round trip through the hills to Goose Creek. Someone had to hunt the horses from the woods range to pull the hay wagons. The wagon wheels had to be soaked in the creek; the summer days had dried out and shrunk the wooden wheels, and rolling over rough places in the roads would loosen them from the metal tires, leaving us stranded in the woods.

There must be at least two coal-oil lanterns cleaned and filled with oil. An ax must be taken along to cut any fallen tree in the road. The roads were not traveled frequently and there was often a fallen tree in the road, with no way around it. We had to collect a hammer and nails and some hay wire for harness repair in case of accident. There were many potential pitfalls, and many precautions to be taken for such a wagon trip through the hills at night.

But by Saturday night, all details had been taken care of and two wagonloads of Baucomites lumbered through the hills to Goose Creek for the spelling match. We pupils, some of our parents, and some outsiders occupied the wagons while older boys and men walked alongside them. Everybody walked up the hills in kindness to the horses; uphill pulling was very hard for range-fed horses.

Iva, Verla and I were perky in new hair ribbons tied in great bows at the backs of our necks; we wore new dresses for the occasion.

Queens of the hayride, we sat in the scented hay which half-filled the wagon beds and absorbed the jar of the wagon over the rocks and hills. Denim-clad boys riding on the sides of the wagon bed surrounded us.

As we neared the little institution of learning that was Goose Creek School, the twinkle of two coal-oil lights on its walls welcomed us.

A raucous crowd met us with a loud, friendly challenge. More denim-clad boys and other girls with fancy hair bows and pretty dresses yelled laughingly, "Strawberry shortcake and huckleberry pie, we can beat Baucom and not half-try!"

We returned their challenge with another cake-and-pie yell in unison:

"Strawberry shortcake and huckleberry pie, V-I-C-T-O-R-Y.

Are we in it? Well, I guess!

Baucom! Baucom! Yes! Yes! Yes!"

Then Uncle Ike Gore drawled with a twinkling smile, "Well, boys and girls, there's one thing about it—you can't eat your cake and

Y is for You
who are going to school,
To learn how to read,
write, and cipher by rule.

have it too." At this, Goose Creekers and Baucomites joined in a good-natured laugh.

The Baucom-Goose Creek spelling match took place only once a year, and since it was an affair wrought with no small amount of hard work in preparation, few ever missed it. The little one-room school was full to running over. There was scarcely room for two groups of the invincible spellers to find standing room along opposite walls and to pass across to the opposite as each called, "Baucom!" or "Goose Creek!" according to the name of his school, and made a "tally."

After the yells, laughing, joking and friendly greetings were over, and the spelling and "tallying" were underway, oldsters sat grimly in the faint, twinkling lights of the lamps, solemnly aware that one of two schools would carry away the honor of the evening.

All was quiet as our Miss Verna and their Miss Ethel first pronounced the word, then used it in context, and then pronounced it a third time, very clearly, out of context. It began to look as if the red-backed book containing the Progressive Course in spelling had been mastered by the spellers.

And then, like a thunderbolt out of a clear sky, our Verla spelled "mesmeric" with two r's and their Ethel spelled it correctly. For a moment the quiet of the room was turned to the sound of exploding bombshells, as Goose Creekers clapped and guffawed.

Then, as if the ice for missing words had been broken and as if guffawing were contagious, their Elsie and their Minnie missed a word each in succession. When tallying time came around again, we were one tally ahead. Just before the two-hour time limit was up, our Willie "turned down" their Earl which, all told, gave us two "tallies" to the good.

With good-natured jibing, much hand-shaking, and hearty invitations for them to return the compliment by coming to Baucom next year, we took our leave.

We gazed on the starry September midnight as our wagons carried us back to the winding waters of our own silvery Baucom, and we saw the milky paths across the sky and the slightly tilted, waning harvest moon which foretold wet, stormy weather soon.

But what a glorious night that night was! ❖

Hot-Lunch Program

Also we lived could take potatoes to bake on top of furnace. What a wonderful smell for dinner.

By Norma J. Hebel

This is exactly what my friend Jaise, Two biggest girls did in forenoons usually cream potatoe with carrots + onions all had hot lunch!

During the 1930s, I lived on a farm in the Ozark Mountains of southern Missouri.

Across the field from our house was the one-room schoolhouse that served our community. However, it was not red; ours was white. It had one large room, with a narrow entrance hall with shelves at one end for our caps and gloves. There were hooks on the wall for our coats. The room was heated with a round wood stove in the center of the room.

When I was in the fifth or sixth grade, some schools started having a hot-lunch program. Our school became eligible for government com-modities. We got oatmeal, raisins, cornmeal, dry beans, butter, canned peaches, canned tomatoes and probably other foods that I don't remember.

We stored the butter on the shelves in the hall where it was cold. The other supplies were stored on a couple of shelves the teacher cleared of books. The rest she stacked on the floor at the side of the room.

When the pupils started arriving in the morning, the older girls were put to work peeling vegetables if we were to have soup that day. We usually had either vegetable soup or beans. Sometimes a parent would send a soup bone for our soup pot. If we did not have meat for seasoning, the teacher used butter. Parents helped with vegetables from their cellars and canned food. Every Monday we brought a few pennies and the teacher bought crackers. We always had butter for our crackers. One mother who lived nearby made corn bread occasionally when we were having beans.

One day a board member came for lunch to see how the hot-lunch program was going. He brought a quart of thick cream to go on our peaches for dessert that day.

My first memory of oatmeal cookies is of those made by the teacher's mother. She used some of the oatmeal, raisins and butter from the commodities and made a large batch. In fact, our teacher told us she got so tired of dropping cookies that she spread the batter in the pan and baked it that way, then cut it into squares. I still remember how delicious they were.

I'm sure today that teaching eight grades and cooking a hot lunch on a wood stove would be considered an impossible task. ❖

When the pupils started arriving in the morning, the older girls were put to work peeling vegetables if we were to have soup that day.

School Days in Winter

By Alma M. Lothamer

While sitting by my front window one winter morning, I could see the children going to the grammar school across the corner. Although it was cold and snowy, most of the boys and girls had their coats thrown open, were without caps or boots, and carried no lunch pails. The scene was quite a contrast to my own school days when I was so bundled up with clothing that I could scarcely see or freely move. Of course, these children walk only a few blocks; those who live at greater distance are driven by bus or car. In my day everyone walked, regardless of how many miles they lived from school.

I grew up on a farm in Michigan, and in September 1915, when I was nearly 7, I began the primer class. It was a 2-mile walk each way to the Scotch Settlement School in Dearborn Township, and so I wore plenty of warm clothing. The open fields made it seem colder and it was not uncommon for the temperature to be down around zero. On those days I wore a heavy sweater under my coat and a woolen cap with matching scarf. I also tied a net fascinator across my forehead, crossed it and brought it back around over my cheeks and chin, where I crossed it once more and tied it behind my neck. I wore long black stockings with knee-length leggings and high-buckled overshoes.

My toes tingled and my fingers often got so cold I could hardly feel the handle of my lunch pail.

The sharp, brisk wind made my eyes fill with tears that seemed to freeze to my face as they rolled down my cheeks. My toes tingled and my fingers often got so cold I could hardly feel the handle of my lunch pail.

Many times the snow drifted against the fence as high as the wooden posts along the country road. A hard crust formed across the top and crackled beneath my feet at each step. However, my mother had warned me of the danger of breaking through and not being able to free myself, so I usually stayed in the tracks on the road when I was alone.

During the fall and spring, I rather enjoyed this walk, as I could listen to the birds sing, watch the frogs leaping in and out of the water-filled ditches, watch the squirrels scampering here and there, and see the beauty of nature all around me. However, in the winter it was different.

I longed for the moment when I would come in sight of the schoolhouse, as my legs would tire from trudging through the deep snow and my body, though wrapped in heavy clothing, would be almost numb with cold. Occasionally, when I finally arrived, I would meet with disappointment, for no warmth would be coming from the big round stove. In those days, since there was no janitor, it was the teacher's responsibility to have the fire glowing before the children arrived. But sometimes she had problems getting the coal to ignite and burn properly, and so the room would remain cold until long after the last bell. On those occasions she allowed us to keep our coats on and march single-file up and down the aisles while she played the organ, pumping it with her feet. Sometimes we would sing from our *Knapsack* song books as we marched.

There was no indoor plumbing. The two outbuildings stood on both sides of the school at the far end of the small playground. The woodshed was at one side of the school and the well was between it and the road. A tin cup hung at the side of the iron pump and provided our drinking water. On nice days the children often asked permission to leave the room, but if the teacher sensed it was just to get outdoors, she would refuse. Needless to say, no one except the bigger boys asked to leave during cold, blustery weather, and some were even reluctant to go out during recess or the noon hour.

Oil lamps with reflectors hung on each wall, and the teacher lit them on very dark days. When we had evening entertainment, the teacher would borrow a couple of extra lamps for the occasion. Once when I was sent to the nearest farmhouse to borrow one, I accidentally spilled some of the oil on the new dress my mother had made for the play. I was very worried, but by the time it was my turn to come onstage it had nearly evaporated and could not be seen in the dim light of the lamps.

There were usually about 20 children in the one-room school, from the primer class through the eighth grade. When one of the grades lined up in front of the teacher to recite, it was more interesting to listen to them recite than to study my own lesson at the double desk I shared with another girl.

My fourth-grade teacher would let us make hot chocolate to drink with lunch. She heated the water on top of the stove and we took turns bringing cocoa, sugar and milk from home. She assigned two girls to wash and dry the cups, spoons and pan and put them in the cupboard for the next day.

My sixth-grade teacher liked a hot lunch and she selected me to go to the home nearby where she roomed and pick it up for her. I was excused five minutes early and was therefore often jokingly referred to as "Teacher's pet." I considered it a privilege, even though it took a bit of ingenuity to keep the dishes from sliding off the tray in my eagerness to get it back to the teacher before the food—as well as my hands—got too cold.

Morning walks to school hardly ever varied from day to day, but occasionally I was lucky enough to get a ride home. If an unusually bad blizzard came up during the day, my father would come with our bobsled to pick me up. A few other children would

Other times, when the road was mostly free of snow, Henry Ford would come along in his little maroon coupe and give me a ride.

jump in and we would ride merrily along with sleigh bells jingling and soft straw covering our feet and legs.

Other times, when the road was mostly free of snow, Henry Ford would come along in his little maroon coupe and give me a ride. He and my father had lived on neighboring farms when they were young boys, and so he never passed me by, even if he was headed in the opposite direction. He liked children and could easily discuss topics of interest at their level. He had also attended Scotch Settlement School back in the early 1870s, so he enjoyed the comparison

of the teaching method of his day. *The McGuffey Readers* were his favorites.

During seventh grade, a more modern four-room building was erected a half-mile farther west. Then, in June 1922, my schoolmates and I bade a sad farewell to the little country school that had served the community since 1862. It now stands in Greenfield Village in the city of Dearborn where millions of people from all parts of the world pass by it each year. For them, it is a historical replica brought back to life, but for me it is the very school in which I learned the three Rs years and years ago. ❖

Old Dunk

By Harlo F. Decker

We lived in the sand hills of northwestern Nebraska—as Dad said, about 40 miles north of nowhere. Somehow, Dad had gained control of a big tract of pastureland that was sparsely covered with grass. (Dad always said he came from a family of people who could fall in the sewer and come out smelling like a rose.)

At one time, a mining company had planned to market lignite there. They had built a good house, put down a well, and installed a windmill that not only pumped water, but generated enough electricity for very limited household needs. Dad was the caretaker of the setup.

When the mining company suddenly lost interest, we were left holding the bag. It proved, however, to be quite a sack. Dad got control of the whole shebang, almost as a gift. I think that proved Dad's insistence about his hereditary lucky star. Those thousands of acres would pasture about one goat to the acre. We weren't too interested in goats, except a few for our own use. (After one gets used to it, goat milk is great; we seven kids had no trouble along that line.) Farmers from the good farming country to the south brought herds of cattle and horses to pasture on our land. That well must have been a good one; those hundreds of cattle drank from it daily and there was always enough, even to water our small vegetable garden.

He was the offspring of a jenny mother and a mustang stallion.

The one big problem was school. We had to ride more than 5 miles to the little one-room school. Actually, that wasn't much of a problem either. We had our choice of a pony, a buckboard and any number of horses to pull it. But I rode Old Dunk by choice.

"Dunk" was for donkey; he was the offspring of a jenny mother and a mustang stallion.

Old Dunk was blind. A scourge of pinkeye had swept the country, leaving a lot of blind and half-blind horses and mules in its wake. I could have had any other mount, but Old Dunk had been my choice before he went blind. Then, he had been ornery, bullheaded and mean.

But now he was entirely dependent upon me. With his ears laid back, he seemingly was his old ornery self, but I knew different. He was listening for guidance.

He had been one of the best jumpers, and not every kid wanted to race me when I rode him. Old Dunk had a desire to win and quite often did. Now that desire was supposedly gone; everyone knew that Old Dunk was totally blind. However, he would still jump the gate when I asked him to. He couldn't see it. He just jumped as high and far as he could when I lifted the reins and said, "Up, Dunk."

Practically all of the kids rode, and after school we would race. They had forgotten that before Old Dunk went blind, they were careful about challenging him. Now he was "Old Dunk" and not to be feared. Now they often said, "Come on, Harlo, git your old cow and let's race."

I, of course, had no pert answer. Old Dunk was no longer a competitor.

Nancy Becker, a girl about my age who had often gone out of her way to be friendly with me, came and whispered in my ear. I paid no attention. Girls were dumb. Why should I listen to her? Nancy, however, wasn't going to be put off. At last I was forced to listen. Maybe girls weren't so dumb after all.

Nancy talked about her plan to a number of kids. No one ever gets anything straight. Everyone got it that I had said this and that. Nancy had only said Dunk would do what no other pony would do.

After school that afternoon, when the kids got their mounts and began to show off, they got kind of loud.

"Come on, Harlo. Git your old cow and show him off."

I wasn't in any hurry. I knew that Nancy's plan was going to work.

At last I made a mark in the sand with my toe, mounted, and rode toward it on a run. At the proper place, I lifted the reins and said, "Up, Dunk."

Thinking that there was a ditch or a gate, he jumped as high and as far as he could. "Now," I said, "let's see your big-stuff horses do that."

They all tried but all failed. A pony couldn't be expected to jump something that wasn't there, or so reasoned all of their mounts (if horses and ponies can reason). At any rate, they all refused to jump.

Again and again I demonstrated that Dunk could and would do it. I had known all along that Dunk would do it. But I did have to revise my thinking about girls. At least, Nancy Becker was just something else to me from then on. ❖

The Old Kid-Hack

By Emma B. Lee

For years I have been trying to find someone who has ridden in the kind of school bus I rode in during first grade back in 1918–1919. We didn't call it a school bus; it was the "kid-hack," and it was pulled by two horses.

I lived on 71st Street, just outside of Indianapolis. Our house was the first house west of Spring Mill Road.

I went to school at Nora, at 86th Street and State Road 37; both roads were gravel and mostly had just two wheel tracks. When two vehicles met on those roads, one had to pull over and wait for the other to pass. Nora must have been 5 or 6 miles from home. Can you imagine riding that far every morning and evening in a wagon pulled by horses?

The kid-hack was an extra-big, enclosed wagon. It had windows all around that could be pushed up like house windows to let some air in during warm weather. The front was all glass at the top, and below the glass was a little slot through which the lines for the horses were pulled.

The driver sat in a chair much like a car seat on the left side at the front. The kids' seats were plain, wide boards on each side of the wagon. There was a door on the side by the driver's seat and another in the back of the hack for the kids to use.

The only heat we had came from one of those little, round kerosene heaters that was anchored behind the driver's seat. That didn't make much heat for a wagon big enough to haul 18–20 kids.

To keep warm, we wore long underwear, heavy woolen stockings, high-top shoes and four-buckle overshoes. In really cold weather we wore sweaters under our heavy coats, warm toboggans and woolen gloves or mittens.

At one time it was the fashion to wear overshoes with the buckles unbuckled and flopping. Of course, our parents didn't go for that, so we unbuckled them after we got on the kid-hack. Then, in the evening, we buckled them up again before we got off at home.

The second year I went to school, and for several years after that, we had a motorized kid-hack. It was built much like the wagon, with glass all around and the backdoor for the kids. It also had boards along the sides for seats, but they had just a little padding.

I don't remember when they started using buses much like today's school buses, but I did ride in a regular school bus the last couple of years that I was in grade school.

I have found many people who walked to school or rode a horse or drove a horse and buggy. But I have not found anyone else who rode in horse-drawn buses except my older brother and sisters. No one else seems to know what I'm talking about when I say anything about the kid-hack. That surely dates me, doesn't it? ❖

Rural School in Wisconsin

By R. Chris Halla

When autumn winds blow through our hair, lift the skirts of secretaries and rattle the pants of fat men going about their daily business; when hickory nuts and acorns fill the ditches along country roads, making it easy for farmers and squirrels to gather them, our minds sense nostalgia in the air and travel backward.

My own thoughts go to a one-room schoolhouse just outside of a small village on the Fox River, where I received my first-, second- and third-grade education, and I am always saddened to think that such buildings no longer serve the noble purpose they once did.

Until the late '50s, the Wisconsin countryside was dotted with rural one- and two-room schools, often no more than a few miles apart. Mostly they are small buildings in small towns or at the fenced-off end of a cornfield, where country road and state highway intersect. Now they are empty, or are put to some little use as community centers. One recalls, though, when out early these autumn mornings, looking through the windows of the buildings, what it was like not so many years ago when school was in session.

Children in groups of three and four, or two special friends, and occasionally a lone child, scuffed along the gravel roadside on their way to school. A bell above the entrance called them. Their hands and pockets were full: Davy Crockett and Hopalong Cassidy lunch boxes, and brown papers sacks, dried leaves and a dead bat for show and tell.

Boys and girls entered the school through separate doors. Inside they were further separated by size in cloakrooms circled by two rows of hooks: the upper row beyond the reach of smaller children. Every day in the little school was divided by a mid-morning milk break, lunch and recess, nearly an hour long, and a 15-minute mid-afternoon recess.

Holidays were almost totally uninterrupted by schoolwork, and it was a rare holiday that passed uncelebrated: Halloween, Thanksgiving, Christmas, Lincoln's birthday, Valentine's Day, St. Patrick's Day and May Day. It seems as though the list never ended. Every holiday had its own decorations, its own radio programs and games, its own songs and decorated cookies and candies.

The crowning event of the school year was the last-school-day picnic in which the entire town and outlying farmers participated.

The crowning event of the school year was the last-school-day picnic in which the entire town and outlying farmers participated. Here child and adult, farmer and factory worker, fisherman and executive, ate and played games together and reaffirmed themselves as a community of friends.

Now these scenes which were enacted in and around the rural schoolhouse are simply memories that we nostalgically recall in our mind's eye. But the human mind is more vulnerable at some times than others. While standing outside the window at Skeleton Bridge School, one can almost hear classes being carried on behind the boarded window and double-locked door as they were years ago.❖

Dear Old Golden Rule Days

By Martha Shilling

Editor's Note: Even though the rest of our memories are about country schools, I thought it only fair to include a representative pair of stories about school in the city. These urban reminiscences remind us that those Golden Rule Days were special wherever we went to school.
—KT

Our lives were first touched by school days when my sister, Mary, was enrolled in first grade in Friends School in September 1913. We were living in a second-floor apartment in Baltimore which overlooked a park and reservoir. My cousin, Mary, who was living with us, and the two Huckel boys were also pupils there, so they all trudged the two blocks to Mount Royal Avenue.

The school was operated by the Friends Meeting, and Mrs. Dolwin was its principal.

The first part of every morning was spent in taking lunch orders from the children who had not brought lunch boxes.

Mary's memories are of books of the *Sunbonnet Babies* with sums worked out on their long dresses. Recess was spent in jump rope and tag; when it was bathroom time they were sent in threes to each toilet to speed up the procedure.

The athletic field where the older kids exercised had to be reached by trolley. It was only on Pageant Day that the little ones went there.

Grandmother was still teaching us to write Spencerian hand in lined copybooks, and to figure fractions by cutting up apples.

In 1916 we moved to a house at 12 Englewood Drive. Mary and I loved this house better than any other. All the homes backed onto a community playing field where we sledded in winter and played ball and all sorts of games. My favorite spot in the house was the bay window with window seat, halfway up the stairs.

Mother decided, as we were so far from a school, that Mary would do just as well with a tutor, so Mademoiselle Compeign arrived. Grandmother was still teaching us to write Spencerian hand in lined copybooks, and to figure fractions by cutting up apples. I listened in on the lessons and could parrot "*le maison*, the house; *le jardin*, the garden; *le chien*, the dog" along with Mary.

Grandmother also taught us piano, and I spent many a painful hour practicing *Annie Laurie*.

Mother was deep in Red Cross work as war clouds threatened, and she went into the city with Mrs. Cave and Mrs. Eckert to roll bandages and wrap simulated wounds.

In September 1918 we had to move back into the city as Daddy was commuting daily to Washington. Our new house was at 839 University Park Way, a tall, thin, three-story home in a row with a long, narrow back yard.

Roland Park Country School was just three back yards away, so here Mary was enrolled in fifth grade. Classes were held on outdoor porches with the pupils seated in chairs with large armrests and a drawer underneath for books and supplies. They wore sweaters and felt boots over their shoes and wrapped themselves in steamer rugs during cold weather. Boys were only accepted through fourth grade so Mary's classmates were all girls.

I was so fascinated by the school that I ran

away to join Mary. When I was found by my frantic mother and duly punished, Miss Lamb said I could come (if allowed) anytime, as long as I was quiet.

Mary and I spent long hours in imaginative games, and for one of these we built a castle complete with drawbridge and moat. Mary was allowed to bring the class over at recess to see it, and then all the girls ate their lunches in our back yard.

Daddy was moved back to Washington as general plant manager of the C&P Telephone Company in March 1920. We all went over by train, arriving at the huge station and taking a taxi to the hotel.

We were left in the hotel room while our parents went house hunting. In those days, *Ladies Home Journal* carried a page of paper dolls in every issue, and *Pictorial Revue* had a page of fat Campbell Soup Kids. We cut these out and stored them in Whitman layered candy boxes and acted out whole episodes with them.

After several days, a house was found. The floors were connected with a system of speaking tubes. You blew into a tube and waited for the floor of your choice to answer. We thought this great fun, and after the cook, Ellen, moved in, we drove her crazy blowing, being sure no grown-ups were about to give us a tongue lashing.

The butler's pantry was furnished with a dumbwaiter which connected it to the kitchen below, and we secretly sent that up and down with our dolls on board.

This time brought my introduction to formal education. It was with great excitement and some trepidation that I hooked my new school bag over my shoulder and set off with Mary to the Maret French School. Everything except English was in French, including opening devotions each morning.

Discipline was considered almost more important than scholastics; marks were strictly

In 1931 it was my turn to take my place in the line of white-clad, pink-rose-bearing girls who walked with measured tread to the harp's plunking of **Men of Harlech.**

given. Good work was rewarded on Prize Day with huge leather-bound tomes printed in French which we received with pride but never read.

I was in fourth grade with Miss Frances Ronaldson as room teacher. Our day ran from 9 a.m. to 1 p.m. with recess from 11:20 to 11:30 a.m. We could buy milk, crackers or bouillon and eat in the dining room, but we preferred to go out on the sidewalk and play jacks, jump rope or hopscotch. Miss Ross had very white hair; she taught English and spelling. Years later, at graduation, she told all my guests, "Martha could never spell 'pilgrim'."

Mary's class had military drill led by an officer from Fort Myers. The girls wore ugly uniforms and carried wooden guns.

Despite the fact that most of the girls came from very wealthy homes, they all loved to come to parties at our modest house.

Daddy and Mother went to so much trouble to plan interesting parties, such as candy-making in the basement kitchen, with each girl taking home a box of goodies. Another time a friend of theirs came and drew our silhouettes. There were also tasting and smelling contests and charades.

One Halloween, Daddy went all out, setting up a speaker in a cornstalk; on the wall, a stuffed owl was hung over a lighted moon. Mother talked to Daddy as "Mr. Owl" and he responded through a hookup behind the moon. The girls were fascinated.

Our classmates' parties were catered affairs planned by governesses and we always played musical chairs and pin-the-tail and had party hats and snappers. Mother didn't approve of movies, but sometimes our friends gave a theater party and so I got to see *Sonny Boy*, *Strongheart*, *Little Lord Fauntleroy* (with Mary Pickford as the Little Lord), *America* and others.

We walked to school, a hike of eight or nine long blocks. Kids were not chauffeured everywhere in those days—not even wealthy kids.

Although Mary and I were four years apart, Mother dressed us alike—and we hated it. Sometimes our dresses were different colors but the same pattern. Twice a year a little seamstress named Miss Simpkins came and stayed a week and made all our clothes.

Our hair hung to our waists and was plaited in two braids with ribbons on the ends. Toward the last years in school we wore one braid, turned up and tied with a big black ribbon. For dances we could put it up coronet-style with big tortoiseshell hairpins.

Mrs. Holton was very strict; there was no chewing of gum; no one wore lipstick; and if caught smoking, it was "curtains" for the offender.

For gym we wore navy blue bloomers, white middy blouses, navy ties, navy ribbed long stockings and high white sneakers. In later years, after we got to the gym, we rolled the stockings below the knee and pulled the bloomers up, always remembering to reverse the process before returning to school.

Fire drill was great fun as the school had to be emptied in record time onto neighboring rooftops or the sidewalk. This diversion often saved some unprepared student from disgrace.

There was also a little Italian hurdy-gurdy man who roamed the streets with monkey and organ. We would prevail on him to stand under the study hall windows and play the national anthem and, of course, we all had to stand until Mrs. Holton irately sent some pupil out to send him away.

The fall of 1924, Mother decided to keep me out of school. I had had some teeth pulled with ether and "looked peaked," she said, probably what they now peg as rheumatic fever or mono.

I was disgusted to be kept home, but decided to make the best of the enforced vacation. I learned quite a few extracurricular subjects from Mother, such as cooking, sewing, ironing, budgeting and general household management.

It was good I was home because Mother suffered a breakdown that spring. The doctor prescribed two weeks at Wardman Park Hotel and two at the Traymore in Atlantic City. I was put in charge of tickets, luggage, etc., and felt very grown-up, if not completely happy with Mother sick.

I would order meals served in our rooms. When she napped I could walk the Peacock Alley in the hotel, or on the boardwalk.

It was then that I learned to store up funny stories to make her laugh. She grew well again and we returned in triumph.

The following fall I was placed in the Colonial School where I was to cram up to be able to return to Holton. Mary graduated that June, wearing a beautiful white eyelet dress and carrying pink roses.

There was no chewing of gum; no one wore lipstick; and if caught smoking, it was "curtains" for the offender.

Her class was one of the few to wear short dresses for graduation. This was during the years that Mrs. Coolidge was wearing short gowns in the White House. Everyone applauded when Mrs. Holton tied her *cum laude* key around Mary's neck, and she sat as one of the favorites on the platform.

In 1931 it was my turn to take my place in the line of white-clad, pink-rose-bearing girls who walked with measured tread to the harp's plunking of *Men of Harlech*. The study hall had been converted with a platform built across the desks, potted palms and ferns; family and friends perched on rented gilt chairs.

I was one of the favored few to sit near Mrs. Holton as she gave us her final eulogy and handed out real diplomas tied in blue and white.

We indeed felt we had reached a plateau as we grasped flowers and diploma, with the fading afternoon light glinting on our senior rings. ❖

The ABCs of P.S. 27

By Rita M. Daly

From 1934–1940, I attended elementary school in New York City. Public School 27 was a large gray building with a green dome. High above the dome flew an American flag. A tall, black, iron fence surrounded the paved school yard. Most of the teachers were women and most of them were pretty old—probably 30-something.

What I remember most vividly about the six years I attended P.S. 27 were the ABCs.

A was for Assembly. Every Friday morning we had assembly. The girls wore white middy blouses and the boys wore white shirts. We all wore blue ties, except on special assembly days. Special assemblies were any assembly that the principal deemed special; then we wore red ties.

B was for Blackboard. Blackboards were very important. The teacher wrote on them. Those who were chosen were allowed to erase what she had written. Some teachers even drew on them, but they all used school chalk.

C was for Chalk. School chalk deserves its own category. When a pupil was called upon to write on the blackboard, it was an honor, an honor mixed with fear—fear that you might make the chalk squeak. Teachers did not like it when the chalk squeaked.

> *C was for Chalk. I loved the school chalk. I used to ask Santa to put school chalk in my Christmas stocking.*

School chalk was special. It was hard; it was not like the chalk I could buy at Woolworth's. I loved school chalk. I used to ask Santa to put school chalk in my Christmas stocking.

D was for Desks. School desks were unique. They had a narrow groove at the top so that our pencils would not roll off. Desks also had a little hole in the upper right-hand corner that held a small glass inkwell. When we reached third grade, the ink monitor filled our inkwells with ink.

Beneath the desk was a compartment to store books. We had to clean out this compartment every Friday afternoon.

E was for Eraser. There were two kinds of erasers in P.S. 27. One was on top of a pencil. This eraser was never, ever used. The teacher wanted to know what mistakes we had made.

The second kind of eraser was the blackboard eraser. These were cleaned every Friday afternoon by the blackboard monitors to eliminate the chalk dust.

F was for Friday. All important events took place on Fridays.

G was for Geography. Geography was a subject taught by the teacher using a flat map that was pulled down like a window shade. With the aid of a long pointer, the teacher then convinced the pupils the world was round.

H was for Hands. Hands spoke volumes. We held them folded in front of us, clasped behind our backs, placed on top of our heads and raised in the air. Their position indicated whether we were being quiet or being punished, or whether we had to go to the lavatory. When we waved our upstretched hands, it signified that we knew the answer to the question being asked.

I was for Ink. School ink was always blue-black. No one knew why. Inkwells were filled by the ink monitors. Ink monitors were always boys. They did not have to be tall. Ink monitors were looked up to by the rest of the class.

M was for Milk. Milk monitors were usually girls. Their job was to collect a nickel every Friday from the pupils who wanted to buy milk the following week.

Each morning at 10 o'clock they handed out the little square containers of milk and white straws to the children who paid their nickel. Some children ordered chocolate milk. That cost a penny more.

P was for Paper. Paper came in two colors—white and yellow. All paper was lined, except drawing paper, which was white.

R was for Recess. Recess was the short period every day when pupils were taken out to the school yard. There we were allowed to run around, play ball, hopscotch or jump rope. Some pupils just stood next to the teacher. These pupils were usually girls.

S was for Silence. Silence was what we had to maintain when the principal visited our classroom, or during fire drills.

T was for Tests. There were three kinds of tests: the oral test; a daily test, always on yellow paper; and a weekly test, always on Friday and always on white paper.

W was for Windows. Windows in the classrooms were about 10-feet tall. They were opened and closed by the window monitor under the direct supervision of the teacher. Window monitors were also responsible for raising and lowering the shades. These important functions were always performed by a tall boy. He ranked right up there with the ink monitor.

Many years later I returned to P.S. 27. The large gray building seemed to have shrunk. The dome was still green and the flag still waved proudly, but it no longer reached the clouds.

When I entered my first-grade classroom I felt like Gulliver entering the Lilliputian world. My beloved desk looked like a dollhouse miniature. With misty eyes I returned to the narrow halls and left P.S. 27 for the last time.❖

Marms, Masters and Other Friends

Marms, masters and other friends helped all of us through our years of education back in the Good Old Days. However, sometimes I think we schoolchildren may have had as great an influence on their lives as they have had on ours.

When I think of the teachers who tried to round off a few of my rough edges, I remember my prim and proper fourth-grade teacher. The memory always makes me smile.

Grandma Stamps was a profound influence on my life in many ways. She explained the deeper mysteries of life like why the morning glories close up with the heat of the day. She laid the groundwork for good nutrition and healthy living. ("Eat your peas—and if you touch my snuff can again, if it don't stunt your growth, I will!") One of the ways she influenced me was in my early speech patterns, sometimes to the chagrin of parents and, later, teachers.

As a big, strapping boy of 8 entering the fourth grade, I encountered a teacher unaccustomed to the country dialect of her charges. Headed out to heed the call of nature one rainy autumn morning, I explained to her that I needed to go but that I would be back "dreckly."

"Dreckly?" she retorted. "What is dreckly?"

"You know, I'll be back pretty quick, soon—dreckly!" I wasn't going to be disrespectful, but my need to get to the backhouse was quickly overshadowing my need to explain the finer points of hill-folk speech. Finally she relented and I hurried out of the room.

"Grandma Stamps always said "dreckly," I explained to my teacher when I returned to the building. After some thought and discussion, she ascertained that Grandma and I were saying "directly." "You meant to say you would be back di-rect-ly," she enunciated.

"What's that mean?" I countered.

"You know, pretty quick, soon—dreckly!" she said in frustration.

The year with that school marm was a challenge to both of us. She was constantly waging a battle to understand some of my phraseology—and to change what she could. She explained that a "fur piece" was a lady's wrap, not a long way to walk. She took out a map of the area to point out to me that my favorite swimming hole was on Barren Fork, not "Barn Fork," as I had learned it. She squinted, frowned and tapped her foot through many of Grandma's little malapropisms brought to school in the form of this stubborn little country kid.

I suppose she was the first step in my loss of Grandma's influence in that part of my life. Leaving it behind, I think I was made poorer. I never passed any of those Grandmaisms on to my own children. All in the name of good English and grammar—what a pity.

Well, it's pretty warm today. I think I'll mosey on down to that swimming hole on Barn Fork. It's a fur piece, but I reckon I'll be there dreckly.

There are a few things I'll probably hang on to the rest of my life—despite all the hard work of those marms, masters and other friends in my little country schoolhouse.

—Ken Tate

Massachusetts Schoolmarm

By Walter Keene

On that morning so many years ago, when I awakened and looked out the window, visibility was zero. A heavy fog had drifted in from Moosehead Lake, the largest body of fresh water in Maine—the largest in New England, for that matter.

The weather matched my dark mood. Fog dripped from the eaves of the house and rested on the grass and flowers. It covered the trees as if a gigantic monster had shed a million tears.

World War I was raging in Europe and there was talk that the United States would soon be involved. My older brother and I were worried for fear that our own dad would have to go. That was another reason I was depressed that day.

But there was something else: It was the day for starting back to school. There was to be a new teacher from Massachusetts; we called teachers "schoolmarms" because they were invariably women. Our school board preferred to import teachers from Boston, that hub of intellectual achievement. The board paid for only a one-way fare from the Bay State for them, because invariably some love-starved lumberjack would marry the teacher and the school board would have to send for another new one.

Every eye was on the new teacher as she faced us. We saw a beautiful Irish girl with big blue eyes.

What would the new schoolmarm be like? Had the school board tired of importing young, unmarried ladies only to lose them to Cupid? Perhaps this year we would have some crabby misfit who would occasionally brandish a stout hickory club and make us do hard sums.

To be sure, school boards considered the ability to "keep order" a prime qualification in a teacher. She usually focused her attention on a small group of pupils—the older boys. Girls were never any trouble. Boys seemed to resent anyone who tried to teach them something. If the older boys could be made to behave, the younger ones would follow suit.

At 9 o'clock that morning, 27 scholars arrived at the schoolhouse. My best friend, Carl, and I had chosen a bench at the rear of the schoolroom. Soon thereafter, one of the girls spotted a team driving up. She quickly left the window and took her seat. A lively scramble followed and those who had not already secured seats, did so.

Every eye was on the new teacher as she faced us. We saw a beautiful Irish girl with big blue eyes and long lashes. She saw a motley group of backwoods children—girls in homemade dresses and boys in overalls. I doubt that she had ever seen such a poorly dressed, mangy-looking roomful of students.

After removing her coat, she began speaking to us in a voice that was soft, low and pleasant to the ear. "In Boston, where I come from, there is a woman who has 20 dogs. People wipe their feet *after* they leave her house. What do you think of that?"

For a moment, we were silent. Then we began to laugh. We laughed and laughed. Then she put up her hand for us to stop. "My name is Kathleen Cronin," she said. "Now, you'll find I'm pretty ignorant of how you do things up here in Maine and you are going to have to help me."

Good Lord, if she had asked any of us boys to turn handsprings, we would have done it!

The oldest girl in school, Dora Crowley, was

She never had a discipline problem because she knew how to handle us. The girls liked her—and the boys loved her.

appointed teacher's helper. She helped Miss Cronin organize our classes; we were all in different grades.

Miss Cronin always started school the same way, by telling us something to make us laugh. How she acquired such a vast repertoire of jokes, I'll never know, but she knew a lot of them and never repeated one.

After the dull routine of chores on the farm, we looked forward to school. We learned a lot, too. She gave frequent tests and we were allowed to take the test papers home, where they were eagerly scanned by our parents. They were very pleased with our glowing reports of our new teacher.

Generally speaking, young folks are glad when school vacation comes, but it wasn't so that winter when Miss Cronin was our teacher. She was an educated girl, but she never looked down on us. She always addressed us as "dear friends."

She would say, "Dear friends, arithmetic is very important. To learn how to add, subtract, multiply and divide will be useful to you all your lives." Sometimes she would conclude our lesson in arithmetic with some little joke:

"Noah took two snakes into the ark, and after the water subsided, these two snakes refused to go forth and multiply. You see, they were adders."

Another day, she said to us: "You will find, as you go through life, that knowledge is your best friend. When your school days are over, keep reading and studying."

One little child raised her hand. She asked, "But you will be with us next year, won't you?"

"No, dear, I'm afraid not," Miss Cronin answered. "Next year I'll be back in school myself at Wellesley College in Massachusetts."

Sadness overcame us. She had become more than a teacher. We regarded her as a wonderful friend.

In January, the weather turned bitterly cold. Walking to school, our feet made that

peculiar crunching noise that comes when the temperature goes below zero.

It was cold in the schoolroom. We older boys kept the little stove stoked with wood, but it wasn't enough to take away the chill. Our teacher had told us to keep our coats on, and we noticed that she shivered and moved nearer the stove.

Festus Potter raised his hand to speak. He was an ungainly youth, almost adult in size, who had never been able to attend school regularly because his folks needed his labor at home. He was a comical fellow and it was a treat to hear him talk.

He began in a bumbling, uncertain, hesitating way, greatly embarrassed. "Miss Cronin," he said, "I've got a nice warm coat that I got from the mail order and I sure would like you to wear it in class today to keep you warm while you're teaching us backwoods folks. That is, if you want to."

"But you need it yourself, Festus."

He replied, "Oh, no Ma'am. I've got two suits of long wool underwear on, one right on top of the other, a flannel shirt, and two sweaters, one right on top of the other."

We began to laugh, but Miss Cronin raised her hand for us to stop. Like the kind, understanding lady she was, she said, "Thank you very much, Festus. I will certainly be very grateful for the loan of your coat today."

She put on the coat, which was far too big for her, and began a discourse on climate and temperature and how much it differed between Massachusetts and northern Maine.

As an afterthought, she added, "We all like a joke, but we must never laugh at the expense of others or say anything that will hurt another's feelings."

That was the way Miss Cronin was. She never had a discipline problem because she knew how to handle us. The girls liked her— and the boys loved her.❖

Teacher's Gift

By Milt Riske

She was the absolute monarch of one of those white, single-room schoolhouses that once dotted the rural landscapes of mid-America. Her subjects were the daughters and sons of the farmers who lived, as the saying went, "too close to ride and too far to walk" from the school.

Any woman with the stern demeanor of Ola Axelford could be called nothing else but "Old Battle-ax." Any teacher who ran so taut a school and kept the upper hand on 30-some live-wire farm kids had to make some enemies.

Miss Axelford's disciplinary domain included a prairie playground, the shed for coal storage, the outdoor water pump, the two small outbuildings used for nature's functions and, of course, the one room for pupils in first through eighth grades.

She appeared domineeringly tall as she paced and pointed out educational facts on the blackboard.

Herein she presided over four straight rows of desks occupied by sometimes-industrious, ofttimes-restless farmers' offspring. Here she observed, discussed and scolded, glowering over—but rarely through—her wire-rimmed spectacles.

She appeared domineeringly tall as she paced and pointed out educational facts on the blackboard with the ever-present wooden pointer.

We thought of her as old, but in retrospect this may have been because we were so young. She was referred to by some in the community, however, as "The old-maid schoolteacher." No one ever called her "Old Battle-ax" within her earshot, though she must have had some idea that it was her nickname.

The older boys sometimes referred to her in more earthy terms on their walks back home and to chores. I, too, had picked up some rather explicit words and joined in.

We were as vehement as only the young can be when their freedom is tempered by authority. All types of dire things were predicted for "one old-maid teacher if I ever get out of the dang school."

Boys, and maybe some of the girls, had carried grudges throughout their school days with Miss Axelford, but once free of her shackles, promptly forgot them. But while we were still in her clutches, she was fair game for our devilish pranks.

On one Halloween, a dead skunk had been placed on the seat of her

Model-T coupe, causing her to drive for several days with the windows open. On another occasion, an emptied box of candy refilled with small bits of coal was a "gift."

I helped select and pay for what we felt was a very appropriate comic valentine for a "slave-driving teacher." Although we sneaked it into the shoe box decorated with red crepe paper and doilies and waited with half joy, half anxiety, as Miss Axelford opened her envelopes with cards and hearts and lace, our envelope was not among them. We never found out what had happened. The boy who was to drop it into the box was accused of "chickening out." A teacher's pet was blamed for tattling to "Old Battle-ax." Quite possibly the teacher was again smarter than her students, and became aware of the plot to embarrass her.

My interest in "getting even" with our adversary slacked for a time when a new interest—a girl, Martha—came into my life. Not that she was new to the school. She had been there as long as I had, from first grade. She had sat near me. We had played games and we had talked. Then, how subtly it changed—a glance, a smile, an awareness. Though she was not a new girl, the feeling I had for her was new.

After I had been sternly rebuked by the teacher for some infraction, I bragged of

I opened my hand and the teacher plucked the note from my sweaty palm. She unfolded the soggy paper, adjusted her glasses, and peered.

revenge. Martha agreed smilingly, "Miss Axelford was sure crabby, all right." I could tell that she was not as sincere as we boys were.

After the great comic valentine plot had misfired and our grade was laboring over an arithmetic test, Martha, seated directly ahead of me, slyly slipped me a folded note. I furtively unfolded it to read.

But we had not perpetrated the pass as secretly as we thought, and the eagle eye of Miss Axelford observed the transaction. The pointer came up with a flourish as a duelist on guard. "Did I see a note passed to you?" she asked me.

I attempted my best air of innocence, but I knew that my burning ears gave away the feigned nonchalance and only a meek "No," slipped around the lump in my throat.

"Old Battle-ax" was out from behind her desk now, striding down the aisle. Her glasses had slipped even lower off the bridge of her nose, and the bun on top of her head made her appear even more menacing.

"Martha, did you pass a note to him?"

Martha appeared to be busily occupied, her nose buried deep in an arithmetic problem. I knew she had heard. Her neck, from the lacy white dress collar to the tips of her ears, burned a fiery pink.

"I know she gave you a note. Probably giving you the answers to those fraction problems you don't seem to comprehend," she continued.

Martha turned her face to the teacher and then toward me. A small tear glistened in each eye.

"Give me the note," Miss Axelford demanded, tapping the pointer on top of my desk. "If you don't I will pick up your papers and fail both of you in arithmetic."

Every face from the desks in front of us stared openmouthed and wide-eyed. Though I could not see behind me, I knew that they, too, watched with anticipation. Martha nodded with helpless surrender, a tear slipping down past her freckled nose.

I opened my hand and the teacher plucked the note from my sweaty palm. She unfolded the soggy paper, adjusted her glasses, and peered.

"Hmm." She reread it. Was it my imagination, or did her lips soften just a little? It could have been the closest thing to a smile that I had noticed on her stern countenance.

"Martha, if your father needs him to help with the chores Saturday, why not just ask him instead of making all this trouble about it?" Folding the note carefully, she handed it back to me.

The test papers were finished and passed in. School was finally over for the day, and once again on our homeward walk we bragged.

"Old Battle-ax sure got fooled today."

"Wasn't that a good one, huh?"

"Sure made her look silly."

"Let me see the note."

"No," I said, "I threw it away. Just about chores when they go away next weekend."

The boys chattered on, but somehow I didn't feel like entering in any longer. In fact, after that I never really felt in the mood to contribute to our little plots.

I read the note when I got home. As I pulled the folded paper from my pocket, I read, "I love you too.—Martha." ❖

The Old Slate

Say, what has become of the little old slate
That we used at school in—say, '98?
The little old slate that was bound with red felt—
And don't you remember how musty it smelt?
Or, maybe that smell that I'm thinking about
Belonged to the sponge that we used to rub out
The words and the numbers we'd awkwardly writ.
(But, some little rascals—my goodness—used spit!)
And then as they dried it—it's hard to believe—
They used nothing less than their hand
or their sleeve!
That seems like a terrible thing to be told—
But things are so different before you are old.
And don't you remember that sharp little sound
The slate pencil made as we scratched around?
And oh, what a SCREECH now
and then we would make—
I'll bet Teacher thought her eardrums would break!

What wouldn't you give to be back in that seat
With your little slate when all life was so sweet?
And wouldn't you like to take back with you too,
That same little happy-eyed gang that you knew?
But I don't believe we would be different men
If we could go back, and start over again.
But oh, if we could, it would surely be great
To start out once more with a new and clean slate.

—Author Unknown

Principal of the Thing

By Alan Sanderson

t's not school that I hate," goes the old joke. "It's the principal of the thing." The "thing" was the brick, two-story school where I obtained my elementary education. For many years, Dorothy Dame reigned indomitably as the principal. Even when I met this grand lady in her office, I was everlastingly impressed by her commanding presence. Of medium, streamlined height, crowned by an upsweep in white, Mrs. Dame projected the authority and disciplined posture of a Marine drill sergeant. A look, a gesture or a word given in reprimand would intimidate the unruliest of boys. Being sent to her office for some display of misconduct wasn't something one looked forward to.

These were qualities I respected at a distance for some time, but upon entering the eighth grade, I quickly discovered that there were many other facets to her magnetic personality. At that time, she also held the lofty position of graduation teacher, and a teacher she was, first and last, in the true sense of the word. She possessed that rare ability of being able to transfer her knowledge to the budding minds of her students in the simplest of terms. Within that framework, I also came to know her warmth, humor, patience and incisiveness, as she spoon-fed me educational nuggets which became a firm base for all my later learning.

Long before the trend toward physical fitness, Mrs. Dame embarked upon her own program.

She was well-versed in any subject she taught, yet Mrs. Dame assumed nothing—especially any information we might have absorbed in the previous seven grades. Her approach was to start with the fundamentals and proceed to the more difficult phases of the course as the year progressed.

Our first arithmetic class had hardly begun when she chalked a double column of figures on the blackboard. Using a wooden pointer to touch each number, she called upon us to add aloud with her. We all started out in confident unison, but toward the end, Mrs. Dame's machine-gun–like voice was the only one to be heard. "Class, you're not with me," she ruefully reminded us. No, I guess we weren't; I'm positive that I wasn't! The best I was ever able to do was accompany her rapid computations for about five digits.

Because I like history, it came a little easier for me. Mrs. Dame enriched me with her detailed accounts of personages I might otherwise have known nothing about. She emphasized people like

Kemal Atatürk of Turkey and Supreme Court Justice Roger B. Taney. They stand out among a score of names which still flash in my mind whenever I reminisce about my last days at that school.

Long before the trend toward physical fitness, Mrs. Dame embarked upon her own program. It didn't matter what the temperature was outside; each day had to begin by throwing open the windows and taking lung-bursting breaths of fresh air. So we wouldn't shiver too much, a series of brisk calisthenics followed. One set of exercises involved rotating of the neck muscles. According to Mrs. Dame, this area of the body was too often overlooked.

With a cheerful smile that triggered a twinkle in her bespectacled eyes, our principal was constantly ready to help any of us with any sort of problem. Indeed, she solved most of them. Those she couldn't solve at least held the attention of her sympathetic ear. Such a teacher forever endears herself to her pupils.

A special way of showing this devotion was to "hang a May basket on her." On a day in that month, a group of boys and girls from the same class would get together and fill a large basket with fruit, candy, potato chips and popcorn. To this was added wide sashes of bright ribbon tied in a bow and a card bearing the teacher's name and the appropriate sentiment.

The basket would be deposited outside the classroom before school began. Then someone would rap loudly on the door. All those in on the basket would run and hide. After the teacher had recovered from the pleasant surprise, she'd delegate three or four of her remaining students to find those responsible. Naturally, all participants couldn't leave school property but, besides showing how we felt, we also had the satisfaction of postponing many a tough test. Mrs. Dame was honored annually, not by one but by several baskets.

If May was for baskets, April was the month in which the graduating class began rehearsals. The program, generally attracting uncounted standees behind many rows of seated spectators, was held on a stage erected in the first-floor hall. It was bad enough having to sit on this platform in uncomfortable new clothes and face such a large audience. On top of that, each of us had a poem to recite from memory at stage center.

My piece was entitled *God, Give Us Men*. The first practice didn't go too well—at least not for me. I'd memorized my lines well enough, but Mrs. Dame said she couldn't hear me beyond the fourth row. She wanted to catch every word distinctly, as she stood behind the last row. When I protested that this was far removed from my capabilities, she suggested that I pretend to be calling for a ball at second base. By June, this bit of self-deception had enabled me to fulfill her request.

My throat went dry. I looked desperately for the help to endure my presentation.

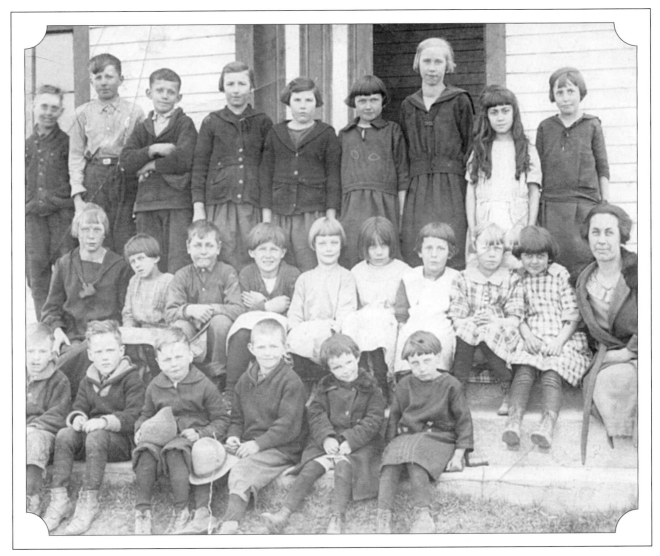

The momentous date finally crawled into being. Our cue to enter the hall was a piano solo. Down the center aisle, behind the smallest girl in the class who led the procession alone, I walked as the male half of the first couple. At a given signal from me, we parted to slowly ascend the stage from opposite ends.

Once seated, I began to sweat out the wait to which I'd been sentenced. I arose rather uncertainly when my time to speak came. As my leaden feet came to a halt at the precise spot, I felt the hushed silence magnify the stares of all those in attendance. My throat went dry. I looked desperately for the help to endure my presentation.

At the last moment, I remembered to glance into the left wing. There, true to her promise, stood Mrs. Dame, wearing a beautiful white dress, a red corsage and a most encouraging smile. I fixed my eyes upon the rear windows and repeated the introduction she had mouthed from the paper clutched in her hand. Sooner than I'd thought possible, I was sitting down amidst the applause. My part was over!

From that point on, I enjoyed myself immensely. The other deliveries and the awarding of diplomas were then a treat to hear. As I retraced my steps down the aisle with my partner, I couldn't help breaking into a joyful trot with the others a few feet from the door. Before I slipped through, however, I wanted a last glimpse of what had been my second home for so long. Instead, my eyes caught the sight of our beaming principal, standing near the edge of the dais, proudly watching another set of her molded children depart toward their destiny. It was only then that I realized the penetrating loss of a great teacher and a good friend. ❖

Old Schoolmarms

I can see the old brick schoolhouse
through the mists of bygone days
Where I struggled with my learnin'
in a muddled mental haze,
And that valiant corps of "schoolmarms"
(bless each patient, faithful way),
How I'd love to thumb the pages
back, and see them all today.

Oh, their work was never easy—
they were martyrs to their trade,
For their job was just commencing
with the groundwork that they laid,
Teaching little hands to "scribble"—
moving elfin minds "to think"—
Making "contact" with the brain cells—
forging "thought chains" link by link
'Til the raw "galoot-like" substance
finally showed a tiny spark
And then flamed upon the tinder
of the soul-engulfing dark.

Do you ever dream you see them—
You who never can go back
To those gold-encompassed school days
down the weather-beaten track
Where, as kids, we played together
at those games we knew so well,
"Getting late" in breathless wonder—
'cause we didn't hear the bell?
An assorted herd of urchins all
stampeding with a rush,
Then, with sharp command, "the ogre"
brought the discord to a hush!

There are echoes from the distance
where those voices once were heard,

There's an odd, nostalgic feeling
for each mellow, muted word,
And I sit in meditation of those
days that could not last,
Weaving rosy robes of fancy for
the shoulders of the past.
Ah, the years have slipped beyond
us—ever moving—ever free—
Leaving pictures to be painted
from an aging memory.

Books are only written records of
the things already done!
To extend that written knowledge
is a goal for everyone!
And the teachers of the nation—
loyal navigators all—
Try to "chart" the course we'll follow—
from the classroom down the hall.
Some will lend unguessed achievement
to the history of the age—
Some will place their own impressions
on the record's printed page.
But, in fancy I go roving through
the mists of bygone days
To a place where once I struggled
in a muddled, mental haze.
Will you harken now, I wonder,
even though it seems quite late
And the "ink of time" is fading
for we soon may "graduate?"
Let me write upon the blackboard
just once more before we part,
"God bless those valiant teachers
from the bottom of my heart!"

—Gordon H. Taggart

Gibson County Truant Officer

By David M. Taylor

G ibson County is the second-largest county in Indiana, in the southwestern part of the state, and Princeton is the county seat, about halfway between Vincennes and Evansville. Princeton has a population of about 7,500.

My dad, Jacob B. Taylor, was the truant officer of Gibson County for more than 20 years, from 1905 until his death in 1927.

He was a tall, rawboned man of 6 foot 2 inches, and weighed about 190 pounds. But he never looked to be that heavy, for he was just muscle and bone and not a pound of fat on him. He was redheaded; he was not a handsome man, but he had a real strong voice that you could hear for quite a distance.

All of that made him quite suitable for the job he had to do. All the schoolchildren feared him enough that they didn't want to play "hooky" from school, because they knew he would be right after them as soon as the teacher reported them to him.

At the time he started that job, there were numerous schools scattered in the country, besides the town schools. Eleven towns had schools, one each in 10 towns and five in Princeton.

He never had an automobile until the last four years of his life, so it was rather difficult for him to get around to all the schools.

He never had an automobile until the last four years of his life, so it was rather difficult for him to get around to all the schools. But he made it anyway, riding a white horse for several years, and then driving an old mule hitched to the buggy or cart. That old mule was as contrary as the days were long. If a piece of paper blew across the road, or a rabbit jumped out in front of him, he would unload you quick! So Dad had to be alert at all times for Old Joe was sure a tricky old mule.

The school kids all got a big thrill out of seeing the truant officer coming to visit their school with that old mule. If he got there while they were in class and they didn't see him, they might be a little noisy or unruly when he walked into their room. But as soon as they saw him, a hush fell on that school. All of those young'uns were mighty good little folks for the duration of his visit, and studied like they never had before.

Dad was quite a humorous man and knew a lot of funny stories that pleased the children and teachers alike. The teachers loved and respected him highly. Knowing his ability to make a good talk on interesting subjects and get off a good joke or two, the teacher always asked him to give a talk. He was never at a loss for something really good to talk about, and when he left the school, he left the kids cheering and laughing.

Dad had five boys of his own in school at one time. That was the first year I went to school; I was the youngest in the family.

His job started at home. He saw to it that his boys went to school. Then he was ready to keep all other children of the county in school.

My oldest brother, Chester, was the only one who ever tried to play hooky. When the teacher told Dad he had missed school, it was just too bad, for Dad would take him out in the yard and warm his pants real good. Then he would stay in school for a long time. But about twice a year that boy just had to try his luck. He always lost, for Dad never gave up on him, and he went on to finish school.

We had to walk a mile and a half to school over a muddy road most of the winter, and lots of days we wore boots or overshoes to school. We lived 6 miles southwest of Princeton, in the Sand Hills, in a little community called Augerville; it was rightly named, for the road had 17 curves and corners in the 11 miles between Princeton and Owensville. Augerville is halfway between the two towns.

There was a general store and several houses that stood close together, and our old schoolhouse, which was called Richland; it also served as our church. Most everyone went to church back at that time. We had some good times in and around that old school.

Dad had to pass that old school every day going to Princeton to his office or other schools, and we didn't know when he would stop in for a visit to see how we boys were doing. Dad was really strict on us boys. Once in a while, some of us would get out of line, and of course a little "peach-tree tea" would straighten us up for a long time.

Some of us would get out of line, and of course a little "peach-tree tea" would straighten us up for a long time.

Being the youngest of the bunch didn't save my old hide a bit, and I can still remember every licking he gave me.

His job wasn't a bed of roses by any means, for he got lots of threats and cursing from both men and women for making them send their children to school. That didn't scare Dad one bit, for he was a fearless man, and they knew he had the law on his side, so they just didn't care to come to blows with him. He never got mad with them; just stated the law and its penalties. The more they threatened or cursed, the more he would laugh at them and just talk nice to them. Before he would leave they would apologize and shake hands and say, "My kids will be in school from now on," and they would be.

Once in a while, one would be mule-headed and not send his kids to school. Then Dad would have to turn the case over to the prosecutor, and after he got through with them and they spent a few days in jail, they were glad to send their children to school.

Anyway, Dad became the best-known man in our county, for he saw kids through school, and then their children. Some of their grandchildren were in school at the time of Dad's death.

I still meet with people from all walks of life who tell me, "I've got your old dad to thank, for if I hadn't been scared to death of him, I wouldn't have gotten an education."

I still thank God for the wonderful dad and mother I had, and count my many blessings. ❖

First-Year Teacher

By A.E. Gray

Sixty-eight years ago I taught my first school. As you may guess, it was a country school—the proverbial "little red schoolhouse"—one room, set near the front of a half-acre plot, and called Turpin School in honor of the oldest and most respected farmers, whose land was adjacent to the school property. Two gravel country roads—one to the east, one to the north—passed the schoolhouse. Of course, there were no school buses and pupils either had to walk to school or be brought by their parents in horse-drawn buggies or wagons. Fortunately, the district was small, so the children did not have to walk too far.

The room was heated by a large, upright, round stove that burned wood. The township trustee saw to it that the wood house outside was well stocked with dry wood for the winter. Drinking water was supplied by a well in front of the building with a tin cup hanging on the iron pump.

During recesses not only did I play, I also was umpire, referee and general "factotem" for settling arguments.

These were the times when railroads were prosperous, with both freight and passenger trains doing a good business. Also, this was the heyday for tramps and hoboes—nomadic, restless men out of work, or avoiding it, who took to the railroads, stealing rides in empty boxcars, subsisting by begging from house to house.

A half-mile across the fields from the schoolhouse was the railroad, a branch of the New York Central, running from Indianapolis into Illinois. The tramps saw our schoolhouse and often, when I got there, I found the building nice and warm as they had slept there and kept the fire going. I was very thankful for this, especially when the weather was cold. The word "vandalism" was not common as it is today. The tramps, no doubt, were so glad for a warm place to sleep that they never did any damage. I only noticed a few missing apples from my desk.

Turpin School was 3 miles from my home, so I had to walk to the school and back home again after school. I walked along the railroad, and often I placed a handkerchief over my face for protection from the cold wind.

Some days I was lucky enough to get a ride on the section crew's handcar, one of the "pump" kind and, of course, I pumped my share, glad for the ride and glad to keep warm. After I got off the handcar, I

walked across the wide field to the schoolhouse. When the snow was deep, it was pretty tough going.

There were two 15-minute recesses, mornings and afternoons, and one hour at noon for lunch. Back in those days there were no hot lunches served in a cafeteria, so children brought their lunches in paper bags or lunch boxes.

During recesses and lunchtime we played our games. I say "we," for I was the biggest duck in the puddle when games started. Not only did I play, I also was umpire, referee and general factotem for settling arguments.

I think the most popular game, especially at noon, was "Scrub," a baseball game in which both boys and girls took part. Instead of choosing up sides, everyone yelled out the position they wanted, starting, of course, with batter. I was the arbiter, deciding whose voice I heard first. We used "string" balls made by the pupils at home by saving up string and wrapping it around a small, rubber ball until it reached the right size, then "sewing" the entire ball to hold the string wrapping in place. It was remarkable how well a string ball lasted, even with batting.

What was the pay in those early days? Well, I got the magnificent salary of $72 a month—

quite a contrast to what a teacher gets today, even discounting the buying power of a dollar, then and now.

Some country schoolhouses had a bell in a little belfry atop the building. Turpin did not have one, so I used a hand bell to call the children to classes. This bell was given to me by my grandmother in 1905, and is well over 100 years old. She told me that one of her sisters, who had been a country schoolteacher in southern Indiana, had used it as a school bell. ❖

There were no hot lunches served in a cafeteria, so children brought their lunches in paper bags or lunch boxes.

Miss Baker Brought Music

By Lorene Ann Clark

*S*he was small and slender, trim and neat, with fine bones and features. An excellent seamstress, she sewed her own dresses and chose bright, bold colors to set off her black hair. Music and art were her specialties. The verse she wrote in my autograph book illustrated her philosophy of life and work:

"Don't B♯ (sharp)
Don't B♭ (flat)
B♮." (natural)

In her own natural way, without any pretense, she taught in Bremen, Ind., in the 1930s and 1940s when I attended school. Her name was Justine Baker.

All 12 grades were Miss Baker's province, for her schedule included going to each elementary schoolroom for an art period and a music period. In the high school, she taught the music groups—"glee clubs," they were called in early years—and advanced art classes.

Mother had to sew a costume for me so I could look just right as I joined in the opening number and the grand finale.

One of Miss Baker's responsibilities was the yearly operetta. She not only supervised the music, but also designed and painted sets for this production. My brother-in-law, Bud BonDurant, had a number of leading roles in the operettas. I always managed to qualify for the chorus, which meant Mother had to sew a costume for me so I could look just right as I joined in the opening number and the grand finale.

In addition to her school duties, Miss Baker provided music for various local club meetings. "Idle hands are the devil's workshop," was never whispered about Miss Baker!

Miss Baker's shining hour came near the end of the school year. Each spring, all 12 grades participated in a huge musical event. Practically everyone in town attended this production—mothers, fathers, uncles, aunts and "cousins by the dozens"—for almost every child in the area was connected with it in one way or another. It took months of planning and preparation. Each grade sang a song or two, a few of the more talented youngsters sang solos, and the entire ensemble joined in some choruses.

The opening number was always the same, with the whole motley crew, from the shyest pupil in first grade to the biggest rowdy in 12th grade, standing and singing out in his best voice: "Welcome, sweet spring-time, We greet thee in song ..."

The tune was *Melody in F*, but to any boy or girl who ever participated in the yearly recital, it ever remained *Welcome, Sweet Springtime.*

Other old standards (remember?) were *Stars of the Summer Night, Drink to Me Only With Thine Eyes*, and *There's Music in the Air*, and also, *Fairest Lord Jesus, America the Beautiful, Battle Hymn of the Republic* and *Columbia, the Gem of the Ocean.*

Humorous selections were included, such as *Froggie Went a-Courtin'* and *The Doughnut Song*. This last one was sung to the rousing tune of *Turkey in the Straw* and elicited chuckles from the audience, who were attentive but uncomfortable on their hard, wooden folding chairs:

"Oh, I went to town
And I walked around the block,
And I walked right into a baker shop;
I picked three doughnuts out of the grease,
And I handed the lady a five-cent piece;
She looked at the nickel and she looked at me,
Said she, 'This nickel's no good to me;
There's a hole in the middle and
It's all the way through.'
Said I, 'There's a hole in your doughnuts, too!' "

The musical evening closed with a sentimental number which brought a tear to the

eyes of the listeners as the youthful voices sang the sweet, sad words of *Smilin' Through*:

"There's a little brown lane
Winding over the hill
To a little white cot' by the sea. ..."

And so the spring festival of music ended. But its echoes remain and the notes sound clearer with each passing year. We smile through misty eyes as we remember how Miss Baker brought music to our hearts and lives in Bremen, Ind., many years ago. ❖

School Will Now Come to Order!

By the Hon. Hugh P. Williamson

During all of the many years that my grandfather, John Williamson, taught our district school in Carroll County, there was order and discipline. He had, when he chose to employ it, an imperious quality of command that secured instant obedience even from the most surly and recalcitrant. After 1887, he ceased to teach, and there followed a succession of masters whose tenures were brief and unhappy.

The school was large, with an average attendance between 45 and 50 scholars, some 12 or 15 of whom were full-grown men, 18–20 years of age, with backgrounds rough and hard. All of them were full to the brim of the restless, questing, daring spirit of youth.

They were a difficult group to handle. One teacher they dunked in the creek and nearly drowned. Another they tied to a tree in the schoolyard, where he would doubtless have remained through a chilly November night had not a passerby released him. A third they pelted with mud, rocks and snowballs until he fled in mortal terror.

By the fall of 1890, the school's reputation had become so bad and so widespread that no one applied for the position of teacher, although under normal conditions there would have been 12 to 15 applicants. The board then bestirred itself to induce someone to come and teach, but it was wholly unsuccessful. It seemed that the district school would not function that year.

Opening day, the first Monday in September, came and went, and no smoke arose from the schoolhouse chimney.

Opening day, the first Monday in September, came and went, and no smoke arose from the schoolhouse chimney; no eager feet hurried through the building; no young voices broke the silence that brooded over it. This state of affairs continued until the latter part of October.

It was about midmorning of Oct. 26 that a short, slender, pale-faced young man, not more than 25 years old, came walking up the path to the home of John Williamson, who was president of the school board. His movements were controlled and deliberate. His voice was calm, level and unconcerned; his manner was mild. His pale blue eyes, wholly without expression, looked like marbles stuck in his head. But despite his slight physique and apparent fragility, there was about him an air of dignity, and in some indefinable way, he conveyed the impression that somewhere in him was an unexpected strength and resolution.

He told John Williamson that his name was Rupert Young, that he

had heard there was a vacancy in the local school, and that he wanted to apply for it. He went on to say he had heard the school was "a little rough," but that he did not believe he would have any trouble. Without inquiry as to his place of origin, experience or educational qualifications, he was hired at once.

On the following Monday morning, many scholars were on the paths and roads that converged upon the school. The rebel element among them, proud of its reputation for toughness, was bent upon making the career of the new teacher short and hard; others, more law-abiding or more timid, were eager to witness the inevitable conflict; a few, no doubt, welcomed the opportunity to advance their education.

By 8:30, nearly 60 pupils had assembled and were milling about the old schoolhouse. Many of them were nearly full-grown. To the slender, pale-faced young teacher who was now seen

approaching down the road, they must have looked formidable. He came up to the group on foot, with a few books under his arm. Nodding, he smiled pleasantly and passed into the building. Some malicious giggles from the older girls and a few low whistles from some of the boys followed him; he gave heed to none of it. Then the motley throng piled in after him, and by a conscious effort created a maximum amount of noise and disturbance in getting seated.

After all were settled at the battered desks, there began a deliberate scuffling of feet on the floor, first on one side of the room and then on the other, in irritating alternation. Before them, on the low rostrum, stood the new master. Their derisive gaze traveled upward, from his sturdy but worn boots and wrinkled suit, to the thin face with its pale, expressionless eyes. He looked lonely, defenseless and frightened, with his arms folded awkwardly across his narrow chest.

And so the situation hung, tense, suspended, evil potential action in reluctant abeyance. The man on the rostrum did not speak or move, and his glance was above and beyond the pupils, to the bare east wall of the dingy building. Thus, for a long moment, the master stood.

Then with a movement so rapid that sight could not follow, he drew a pistol from his side pocket, and as it sped upward, fired, with a roar that seemed to fill the room with an unbearable volume of sound. Instinctively, every student's gaze turned to the back of the room where, exactly in the center of the lintel of the door, there appeared a small, round, blackened bullet hole.

> *Then with a movement so rapid that sight could not follow, he drew a pistol from his side pocket.*

Now the master stood with pistol arm extended, the smoking gun in his hand, smoke drifting around him, immovable as a rock. The eyes that had been expressionless gleamed now with a baleful blue fire that struck terror in the heart of the most redoubtable beholder.

And even as the scholars watched, the pistol spat and roared again. Five times in instantaneous succession, the heavy gun spoke, the crashing sound deafening all within the room. Again the looks of the pupils swept back to the lintel of the door, where around the single center hole, and equal distance from it, appeared five bullet holes forming an exact circle. The scholars looked again at the master, who was almost wholly hidden by the blue powder smoke that slowly drifted upward and parted to show again the eyes gleaming with a hellish and evil light.

Slowly, as the light of the sun fades in the western sky when the day is done, the demonic light faded from the eyes of the man on the rostrum. Slowly the hand that held the gun dropped to his side, and the gun was thrust into his pocket, disappearing in its voluminous folds.

Again the master resumed his attitude of languor; again there crept about him an atmosphere of loneliness and fragility; and when he spoke, his voice was low and thin. He said, "School will now come to order." It did, and so it remained.

Master Young proved to be a better-than-average teacher, and during the remainder of that winter season, his pupils made more than a normal amount of progress. Never again did he raise his voice; never again by word or gesture was he other than a frail, lonely, timid figure. He did not need to be. When the term ended in April, he collected his salary and departed—to where, no one knew.

This, however, was not quite the end of the remarkable story of the unusual master, Rupert Young. In the early part of the following July, there appeared at John Williamson's place a man who identified himself as a deputy sheriff from Golden, Colo. He said that he held a warrant for and was seeking a western outlaw named Charles Belt, who sometimes used the alias Rupert Young and who sometimes taught in isolated country schools for brief periods.

This man, the deputy added, was wanted for shooting seven persons; he had robbed numerous banks and had held up several stagecoaches in the West. He said he had heard that a man who might be Young had taught at the district school the past year. His description of the outlaw tallied exactly with that of the departed master. John Williamson was able to tell him only when Young had left. Whether he was ever captured and brought to justice for his crimes in the West was never known in Carroll County.

The district school stood until its destruction by fire in the spring of 1917. The bullet hole in the lintel of the schoolhouse door, with the five holes in a circle around it, was long pointed out, and the story of the master was often told. Never again, in that district, did a teacher have serious trouble with the scholars. Master Young had left an imprint that time did not efface.

The story was told by my grandfather in my presence on a number of occasions, and was repeated from time to time by my father, both of whom are now long since deceased. I have also heard the story repeated by old people in the neighborhood where I grew up. The event occurred about 1895. You may be sure that the story is correct. ❖

Teacher's Exam

This is the grammar section of a teacher's examination from 1886. After successfully completing all sections of the exam, the new teacher was rewarded with a teacher's certificate. One certificate from the 19th Century is printed below.

1. Define grammar. How is it usually divided?
2. Define declension and conjugation.
3. What is tense? Name and define the tenses.
4. Name the classes of pronouns. Decline a personal pronoun.
5. Correct the following sentences and give reasons for the corrections: Who did you sent for? They that help us we should reward.
6. Classify sentences according to structure and give an example of each class.
7. Write a sentence having for its predicate the potential, present perfect, third, plural form of the verb write.
8. What parts of speech admit of comparison? Compare a word from each.
9. Give five rules for the use of capital letters.
10. Write a sentence containing an adjective clause.

Third Grade

PORTAGE COUNTY.

WISCONSIN

COMMON · SCHOOLS

TEACHER'S CERTIFICATE

It is Hereby Certified, That *Miss Katie Campbell* has passed a satisfactory examination upon all points required by Law for a *Third* Grade Certificate, and *she* is Licensed to Teach, in the *County* of *Portage* for *one* year from the date hereof, unless this Certificate is sooner annulled. The following is *her* standing in the several branches upon the scale of 10.

Orthography	7	Grammar	8	Physiology		Algebra	
Orthoepy	8	Geography	8	Theory and Art of		Physical Geography	
Reading	8	United States History	9	Teaching	10	Natural Philosophy	
Penmanship	8	Civil Government	6½	Experience in Terms	4	Geometry	
Arithmetic	9						

October 4th, 1886. *Andrew P. Een,* Co Supt. of Schools.

One-Room Teacher, 1922

By Berniece Van Dusen

The first school I taught was a one-roomer at a crossroads with no one within shouting distance, a miniature country kingdom for a village gal. I was overwhelmed with emotion when my pupils told me how they had come along with their mothers during their summer vacation to clean the building and make everything fresh and bright for our first day together. Thereafter, I never moved in to a school with more sparkling glass, scrubbed woodwork or flawless blackboards. What is more important, I never again found new pupils so glad to introduce me to their school.

Convinced that I was their parents' helper, entrusted with instilling their values of honesty, industry and fair play in their young ones, I truly believed that home, school and church cooperated in the effort.

A beginner didn't necessarily have to apply for her first job in those unbelievable days. Before I had thought about teaching as anything more than a remote possibility, a trustee from an outlying district approached my dad. "I understand that you have a daughter graduating from high school this June. Our district needs a teacher."

It was a little frightening. What did I know about teaching? I had only played school with younger children.

It was a little frightening. What did I know about teaching? I had only played school with younger children. This meant the real thing. What did the trustee know about me? The next day, I sat myself down on the school stairs to learn the multiplication tables my teachers must have believed they had taught to me.

Two other trustees mentioned my teaching to my father. By this time, I had made up my mind that I wouldn't teach near home. Imagine a trustee reporting my beginner's mistakes to my parents! I decided to make my own way. My own mother had been a teacher. So had our stepmother, as well as a grandfather, uncle, aunts and cousins. They believed I could do it. Mother said I'd learn how at summer school right after graduation.

"Don't choose a school with a lot of big boys," I was advised. "Don't pick one, either, near a little store and so avoid the chewing gum and candy problems."

I still had to finish high school and my birthday wasn't until May. The board of education, on which my mother was *the* female member,

purchased a set of new World Books. Since I had already read through the volumes of Stoddard illustrated lectures along with the older Burton Holmes travels, I began these.

Invariably, a well-meaning young teacher, fresh from college, would ask me, "Shouldn't you be doing your algebra or Latin homework?"

"If I can take this book home."

It was news to me that reference books were not allowed outside the building, so I continued to do my math and language at home and to study the encyclopedia during study hall.

I read articles on kindergarten because I planned to teach in one someday. The books were cross-indexed so that at the end of each article I was referred to other similar material in education and in each subject area.

I recalled my own primary teachers drawing number pictures on the chalkboard. Two pictures of trees + two more trees = ? We used to copy the formula, then draw four trees in the empty space. How well I remembered drawing all those stick chairs and houses and circular rabbits and cats that children color today in workbooks or on photocopied sheets.

Directions for constructing paper boxes and baskets reminded me that I used to enjoy that. Not only could I show younger children how, but I would enjoy doing it.

Summer school was a rude shock. After spending hours poring over a school catalog, deciding which classes would be most worth my time and energy, I was told with large red check marks, "You will take this, and this, and this." That was it. At the end of the summer, I had the uneasy feeling that I had probably taken all the wrong subjects.

My efforts to proceed on my own merely transferred the responsibility from my father to his brother, my favorite uncle, who, being a schoolman, knew the procedure.

The trustee to whom he transported me for an interview said, "I do wish you had had some experience." He didn't mean teaching a Sunday school class or helping with a Junior Mission Band at church.

"If everyone says that, how will I ever get any experience?" I replied.

This made him laugh. "She's bigger than my wife was when she started. I'll take her."

It was a relief to have no eighth grade students the first year when I would be teaching beginner's reading, writing and counting. My seventh

Despite my greenhorn bumbling, that first school district is one that I remember fondly.

graders hadn't attained their growth spurts, so I was the biggest person in the room. It distressed me to observe children sitting on their coats and sweaters. In my village school, a cloakroom was always taken for granted. Our hall had a few coat hooks, but not nearly enough, so with trustee permission, I bought some at the hardware, paying for them myself.

I lettered each child's name above a hook, tying on a thin rope with a clothespin to pinch pairs of overshoes or rubbers together. We stored our lunch boxes under the bench that held the water pail and dipper, an arrangement that saddened my germ-conscious sensibilities.

We congratulated ourselves on achieving an orderly classroom—until the beginning of winter when a boy showed us his frozen lunch. That may have been the origin of toasted cheese sandwiches, for all I know, but it ended my makeshift cloakroom until spring.

Cold weather introduced me to the "hot dish"—not a hot lunch at first, but just cocoa or soup to eat with sandwiches from home. My pupils taught me how to bake potatoes on the stovetop under an overturned washbasin. One family, by phone arrangement, would bring a Mason jar of parboiled beans, soaked overnight, to mix with another's quart of farm milk. Sometimes, we had cubed potatoes, carrots and onions mixed with milk, salt, pepper and butter.

At recess, my first pupils would pair me off with their fastest runner for playing "Stealing Sticks," a great game for a school with no playground equipment except the rope swing I had provided. Two teams faced each other across a line scratched in the dirt or snow, the object being to grab a stick from the opposing team without getting tagged to become a prisoner and forfeit the stick. The side having the largest pile at the end, or at bell time, was declared the winner.

Back in the schoolroom, I only needed to say, "Recess is over. Back to work," if anyone tried to take advantage of our recess camaraderie.

At my boarding place, one of the high-school daughters told me, "In the entire eight years I attended your school, no teacher ever had to speak to me regarding my school behavior." I've often wished that ambition had become usual. It should never have gone out of style.

When I watched my pupils construct a pole-vaulting stand, I realized that I was about to experience my first Field Day. They explained the need for practicing running broad jumps and standing jumps, and they marked off space for 50-yard and 100-yard dashes. I used my talents, meantime, to prepare a play for our indoor morning program in the town hall.

Despite my greenhorn bumbling, that first school district is one that I remember fondly, even now when all physical evidence of any building has disappeared. Only the lilacs and sumach that lined the wire fence remain to nod to passing yellow buses. Even the cottage that was remodeled from the buff-colored clapboard school is long gone. When I refer to my former boys and girls, my daughter reminds me that they are gray-haired and nearly as old as I am now. ❖

Teaching in the 1920s

By Charles S. Chamberlin

Recently we have seen big-city teachers' unions strike for higher pay, smaller class size and better fringe benefits, but in the Roaring '20s, when we were happy just to have a job, things were different.

I recently reread an old teachers' contract for a Wisconsin school district, signed in 1922.

"Miss Doe agrees:

1. Not to get married. This contract becomes null and void immediately if the teacher marries.
2. Not to have company with men.
3. To be home between the hours of 8 p.m. and 6 a.m., unless in attendance at a school function.
4. Not to loiter downtown in ice-cream stores.
5. Not to leave town at any time without the permission of the chairman of the Trustees.
6. Not to smoke cigarettes. This contract becomes null and void immediately if the teacher is found smoking.
7. Not to drink beer, wine or whiskey. This contract becomes null and void immediately if the teacher is found drinking beer, wine or whiskey.
8. Not to ride in a carriage or automobile with any man except her brother or father.
9. Not to dress in bright colors.
10. Not to dye her hair.
11. To wear at least two petticoats.
12. Not to wear dresses more than 2 inches above the ankles.
13. To keep the schoolroom clean:
    a. To sweep the classroom floor at least once daily.
    b. To scrub the classroom floor at least once weekly with soap and hot water.
    c. To clean the blackboard at least once daily.
    d. To start the fire at 7 a.m., so that the room will be warm at 8 a.m. when the children arrive.
14. Not to wear face powder, mascara or to paint the lips."

And, by the way, the pay was all of $75 per month!

Leaves From My Diary

By Lola Lamoreux

I have just been through the biggest weekend of my life. Being all worn out today, I am wondering if a city girl should try teaching way out in the sagebrush country where things are so different.

On second thought, perhaps she should. The experience is probably worth a year at normal school for teachers, although I wouldn't know, never having gone to normal school. However, I went to high school for two years and passed my teacher's examinations, so I can't be too ignorant, and I'm sure I look and act more than my 17 years.

Walking home from school on the dusty sagebrush road on Friday, I was so engrossed in reviewing my first week of teaching those eight little kids, I didn't see Hank VanderMeer standing by his barbed-wire gate until he called to me.

"Hey, Teacher," he said, "want to go to the Wood Creek School dance tomorrow night?"

I had met Hank casually one evening when he stopped by the homestead, presumably to visit his sister, but I think secretly to see what I was like. All I really knew about him was that, besides being a tall blond, he was a homesteader and Mrs. VanDusen's brother (I board with the VanDusen family). Mother has always warned me never to make dates with persons I don't know well, so I hesitated. When Hank said his sister and the two girls could go along, I accepted.

I had met Hank casually one evening when he stopped by the homestead, presumably to visit his sister.

Our kitchen was a busy place on Saturday morning. An aroma of warm chocolate cake and fresh apple pies filled the house. Even though I'd just finished breakfast, my mouth watered as I helped make sandwiches with homemade buns, smoked ham and corned beef. "Are we furnishing food for everyone?" I asked Mrs. VanDusen as I put the last slice of ham on a large bun.

"Of course not. Wait till you see what the others bring. It's jist you ain't been to these dances before."

After lunch she brought in the washtub and put it on the kitchen floor. "Time for baths," she said. "Teacher gits the first one. You kids go set in the bedroom and I'll call you when it's your turn."

Baths over, she lit the lamp and placed a curling iron in its chimney, then carefully crimped her own and the girls' hair. Next, the ironing board came out and clothes were pressed.

I was as excited as Amy and Mayme and debated for a long time about which dress to wear. The pink was my newest, but the green with the big brass buttons was the most becoming, so I decided on it. After all, I might meet Prince Charming. (What a joke!)

Long before dark, Hank, dressed in a wrinkled blue serge suit, came in. "Let's git going," he said, picking up the dishpan full of sandwiches. Arms loaded with cake and pies, we followed him out to his old tin-pan auto.

Mile after mile we crept along the narrow, winding road. The auto swayed and jerked, throwing me first against Hank, then over against the opposite door. At nearly every turn, there were big rocks in the road, causing Hank to swerve hastily into the brush to avoid them. We seemed to be either climbing out of a dry wash or rolling into one, and there was always a chuck hole at the bottom. I wondered what would happen if we should have an accident, as there wasn't a homestead or abandoned house along the way. But the auto held up, and after about 25 miles, we came to the Wood Creek School, nestled cozily between two small knolls.

Several families had already arrived and were standing about in the yard visiting. Among them was a small dark girl whom I decided must be the teacher. When she saw us, she came running.

Hank introduced us ceremoniously. "Miss Burns," he said, "let me make you acquainted with our new teacher, Miss Holmes."

We had only been talking for a few minutes when a big lumber wagon drove up. "Let's go in," Miss Burns said. "The Coles are here with the organ. We don't have an organ in our school like you do."

The homesteaders were still arriving. They came in spring wagons, hacks, on horseback and a afoot. We had the only auto. Families alighted carrying children, patchwork quilts, food and coal-oil lamps. I had never seen anything like it, and it made me feel as if I were in another world.

A big fire was started in the yard and a huge black iron kettle, filled with water, was set over it to heat. The organ was unloaded; the lamps were brought in and lit; the desks were pushed against the walls. A big 6-footer entered with a fiddle and a young woman sat down at the organ.

The dance was on—two-steps, circle waltzes, ladies' choice, partners for a square. The two-steps and waltzes were familiar from high-school dances, but I'd never seen a square dance. "It doesn't matter, Teacher," I was told. "Git right in and we'll larn you."

I was whirled and bounced and shaken and passed from one arm to another in rapid succession. And the men! They smelled of onions, of beer, of chewing tobacco and of the barn. My head swam as they grabbed me, stepped on my feet, bowed and scraped, and swung me into the air. Meanwhile a call sang out directions like "Grab your partner, balance and swing, now chase the hobo round the ring!" or "Birds hop in and crows fly out, pluck a gal, and strut about!"

Children ran among the dancers, falling down and picking themselves up—no one paid any attention to them. As the evening wore on, one by one they left the floor and crawled into the quilts laid against the wall and went to sleep.

About midnight, the music stopped. The men wiped their sweaty faces and went out into the yard to make the coffee while the women took over the food that had been placed on the teacher's desk. When the coffee was ready, they passed big mugs of it around to wash down the mountains of food. In no time, that huge pile of sandwiches, cake and pies was gone. Men belched; pipes were lit and tobacco pulled from pockets.

Miss Burns rapped on her desk. "The first guy who spits on the floor will be expelled from school for the rest of the term," she said. Everyone laughed, but those who wanted to chew went outside.

Surely they'll go home now, I thought. I was dead tired; my feet hurt and my legs ached, but no one made a move to go. Instead, the woman who chorded went back to the organ and the fiddler tuned up. The dance was on again with all the zeal of the early evening.

Hank looked confused. "Cut out the big words. Are you going to kiss me or ain't you?"

I asked Hank if they didn't ever go home. He said, "Sure, as soon as it gits light. Why, ain't you having a good time?"

"Oh, yes," I lied, trying to put enthusiasm into my voice.

Hank beamed. "I sure thought you'd like it. We'll go to every dance in the country this winter. You might as well have a good time. You can't be drudging with kids all the time."

Drudging! I'd rather teach a whole month than have to go through another quadrille tonight.

Finally, dawn came and we were on our way home. The sun over the distant mountains made soft pink lights across the sky; the larks sang their early-morning songs as they swung happily on the barbed-wire fences. How serene it was. But no matter how beautiful the day ahead, I was going to sleep it all away (or at least thought I was).

Our little homestead house had never looked more inviting than when Hank stopped his auto before the gate. Mrs. VanDusen and the girls hopped out and went inside.

I started to follow, but Hank grabbed my arm and held me back.

"Teacher," he said softly, "you sure are a sweet girl. How about a kiss before I go?"

I drew myself up with what little dignity I could muster and said in my best schoolteacher voice, "Mr. VanderMeer, I do not indulge in promiscuous kissing."

Hank looked confused. "Cut out the big words. Are you going to kiss me or ain't you?"

"I ain't!" I almost shouted, jerking my arm away and stumbling into the house. I have no recollection of undressing and getting into bed.

Mrs. VanDusen woke us at about 9 a.m.. "Git up girls," she said, "or you'll be late for Sunday school."

"Do we have to go?" I groaned, still half asleep.

"You sure do. Our teachers are expected to help with the Sunday school and you got to go, especially today, because folks here think if the teacher can dance all Saturday night, she can serve the Lord on Sunday."

I didn't want to go, but I didn't want to make the "folks," whoever they were, mad at me either, right at the beginning of the term, so I got up.

We ate a hasty breakfast and started off. Never had the 2 miles seemed so long. I was stiff all over. My head was spinning. … *"Grab your partners, balance and swing, now chase the hobo round the ring."* Over and over, the words raced crazily through my head.

We were a little late, so I slid into the back seat, hoping I wouldn't be noticed. But the leader, a snaggle-toothed, disagreeable-looking woman saw me. She said, "Now that Teacher finally got here, we'll sing number 10. Teacher, you come and play for us."

> *We were a little late, so I slid into the back seat, hoping I wouldn't be noticed.*

I looked at the organ, wondering if my feet would pedal it.

After the hymn, she announced "We will all stand while Teacher leads us in prayer."

I staggered to my feet, stunned. At home I sometimes prayed aloud in Christian Endeavor, if given advance notice so I could think of something suitable to say, but I wasn't prepared for this! My mind kept singing, *"Grab your partners. …"* My face burned. Finally, I stammered: "Oh, Lord, bless us all. Bless those who are here and those who are absent." The room was dead quiet. I couldn't think of anything more to say, so I repeated the exact words again, then added a feeble "Amen."

The snaggle-toothed woman gave me a withering look. "Let us unite in the Lord's Prayer," she said. We sang some more, went to classes, repeated the mizpah, and it was over.

Hank was waiting for me on the porch. "Want a ride home? My cayuse will ride double," he said. I thought those were the most beautiful words I'd ever heard, and if he'd asked me to kiss him then, I guess I would have.

In a very unteacherly fashion, I climbed up behind the saddle. Hardly waiting to thank him when we rode into our yard, I slid off the horse, stumbled into the house and tumbled into bed. And I still haven't decided whether a city girl should teach in the sagebrush homestead country.❖

Egg Case Competition

By Eloise M. Phinney

Back in the '30s we had what might be called "The Summer of the Tent Caterpillar." They were everywhere that year. Trees and bushes were festooned with their clinging, filmy tents filled with voracious caterpillars. Leaves vanished overnight, leaving stark branches as the invaders munched their way across the landscape.

It was the summer when food would be hardly laid out on the picnic table before a creepy, crawling, fuzzy gray worm would try to hide under the leaf lettuce that cradled a mound of potato salad, or perhaps one would be slowly inching up the nearest pitcher of lemonade. They squished underfoot and rode on the screen doors of houses. Even worse was walking under a tree at the swimming hole and suddenly having a horrible scratching feeling going down my bare back!

From the first graders through the eighth, everyone brought egg-case-laden twigs to school.

Ours was a farming community and some of the farmers wrapped rags around the ends of long poles, soaked them in kerosene, lit them and, holding them up to the tents, tried to burn them out. Such a cure could prove dangerous during a dry spell.

Finally, fall and winter came. At last, the caterpillars disappeared and, as far as we schoolchildren were concerned, were quickly forgotten.

However, we hadn't reckoned with our teacher. Mrs. H was a great believer in the learning experience outside of books as well as in the schoolroom, and seized every opportunity to expand our knowledge of the world around us. She felt this would be a good time for us to help rid the countryside of some of the pests and have a nature study lesson at the same time. I doubt if any one of us had ever heard the words "ecology" or "environment," and to us, "conservation" meant planting trees and strip cropping.

So, on a morning in January or February, Mrs. H brought a small brown twig to school. She asked us to pass it around the room and examine it closely. In a one-room school with perhaps 16 students, it didn't take long. We were all puzzled, wondering what new game she had in mind.

But it wasn't a game. Oh, no! Mrs. H had a marvelous idea. We were going to fight the caterpillars. Now we *did* wonder. How could we combat those squirming woolly things in cold weather when there wasn't a sign of them anywhere?

That was where we were wrong, she told us. Hadn't anyone noticed the curious, shiny brown lump on that twig? No one had, feeling one twig looked pretty much like another. But that lump was the egg case of a tent caterpillar. When the weather grew warm, they would hatch and we would be invaded again. The time to clean out at least some of them was now.

How? She was quick to explain. We all walked back and forth to school. Practically everyone passed some low-growing bushes and trees along the way, and there were hedgerows between many of the fields. On many of the small branches were the egg cases. All we had to do was look for them, and when we saw one, break off the twig it was fastened to. What could be simpler?

To add interest, there would be a contest to see who could collect the most egg cases. The contest would end on Arbor Day. We were to bring the twigs to school so they could be counted and a record kept. I believe the branches were kept in the school's woodshed where it was so cold there wasn't any chance of their hatching ahead of time.

How enthusiastic we all were—at first. From the first graders through the eighth, everyone brought egg-case-laden twigs to school. Soon, most of the easy-to-reach bushes were picked fairly clean. Then the snow grew deeper, winter's cold settled in, and it wasn't much fun stopping along the road in the late afternoon to search for those sometimes hard-to-find, shiny lumps. In fact, there were times when the contest dragged to nearly a complete halt—until someone would bring in a new collection and the rest of us would start hunting again.

Most of the time I maintained my sense of competition. There were boys in school bigger than I was (I think I was in the sixth or seventh), and they seemed to assume it would be one of them who would win the contest. That kept me motivated. There were times, after stepping in a snowbank over my galoshes or struggling with a twig reluctant to part with its larger parent, when I was almost ready to concede defeat—almost, but not quite.

Winter finally whiled away and signs of spring began to appear. Arbor Day arrived. Arbor Day was always special at school. It was the day we cleaned, inside and out. Windows were washed and desks were thoroughly cleaned, some for the first time in months. Trash and papers were burned. Since the yard was surrounded by tall pines and hardwoods, we didn't plant trees, but after winter's storms, the yard was littered with small branches. These were gathered and the yard made ready for spring games.

This year of the caterpillar egg contest had a special difference. At last, all the twigs with their egg cases were counted and each total credited to its collector. Then, what a giant bonfire we had, and Mrs. H let us know she was proud of us! She gave all of us the feeling of accomplishing something worthwhile. The satisfying results showed that summer when there were far fewer caterpillars than the year before.

And, what a surprise when I learned I had the largest collection! I still have the candy dish Mrs. H awarded me as the prize.❖

"Dist a Bistit"

By Leona Whorton

In the early '30s, when the entire nation was in the depths of the Depression, and many people were close to each other because of dire need, I taught school in Andrew County, Mo., for the fabulous salary of $90 per month.

Needless to say, I didn't have any luxuries, and couldn't save any money nor drive a new car, but a job was a job. For $18 per month, I had excellent food and a good room, which included a feather bed (now unheard of, but back then a treasured luxury for anyone sleeping in a unheated bedroom). I felt very fortunate indeed, considering the millions who were out of work and hungry, and those who had some work but were still hungry.

There were two distinct classes of people in my community: the people who had plenty of money and were going to keep it, and the very poorest of the poor. Of course, there was a sprinkling of the good old substantial middle class. In contrast to the wealthy, I remember one family of 12 who were trying to eke out a living on $30 per month, the going wage for a farmhand of that day.

Thanks to my mother. I stood by her and cooked from the time I was tall enough to reach a table.

I bought gingham and the club women made six dresses for the family's three girls, and I could manage overalls for Jimmie, but to help with their food seemed beyond me because I had obligations to my own family.

One day, Jimmie ate with me. It was always the custom in my rural school; each child took his turn by the day. I never knew whether a child ate with me because he liked me, or because he was hungry and thought perhaps I would share my lunch with him. The latter was more probably true.

When Jimmie's turn came, he looked at my lunch as I opened it, then looked into his own sack and remarked, "Dist a bistit." That was his lunch! Just a cold biscuit.

Today, with our hot-lunch program in our schools, and evidence of luxury all around us, I'm afraid we have forgotten the Depression years, and Jimmie's story is almost a myth. But back then it was a reality.

On returning to my boarding place that night to a good farm supper, I could not help but wonder what Jimmie had for his supper. His stark remark, "Dist a bistit," haunted me. Before the evening passed, Billy and Mollie Selecman and I were laying plans for an all-out carnival, the funds of which were to be used to establish a hot-lunch program.

The idea caught on fire with the children, and they worked like little Trojans. I sold chances on a double blanket to cover all of the expenses of our "bingo stand" which held an array of dishes, pictures, cooking utensils, bath towels and wash rags.

Each day we could all have all we wanted of one good dish of hot food to supplement the cold lunch of "dist a bistit."

When the big day arrived, Billy, Mollie and I built all the booths in the basement of our one-room rural schoolhouse. Billy could not drive a nail, but he hooked up old Bob and Ribbon to the wagon and brought down the lumber, saw, nails and hammer. Mollie and I set about to build booths of all sorts, many of which would put to shame the "do-it-yourself" jobs of today.

Perhaps the booth housing "The Last Take-Off" afforded as much or more pleasure than any other. This was a very ragged pair of long underwear. It was just as intriguing and fascinating to Bell, the first grader who ran the show, the last time we pulled the curtain as the first time.

Of course, there is usually a bachelor willing to do his bit for the school. We had electric lights, but we needed a long extension cord to light our bingo stand, for the best display of our prizes. An extension cord was brought by Frank, and he placed a light in such a manner that our prizes were shown to their greatest advantage.

At 8 p.m., the curtain rose on a short program that pleased every parent. Why? Because every child had a part in that program. Then we were off to the basement for the carnival. Everyone in attendance gave loyal support. We cleared $32. I bought a hot plate and stashed away the rest of the money for food for hot lunches.

Teaching has always been my profession but cooking has always been my hobby, thanks to my mother. I stood by her and cooked from the time I was tall enough to reach a table.

We thought we had a good one-dish meal when I cooked a big kettle of soup beans, well seasoned with meat and macaroni thrown in for an added vitamins. I had one little girl who said she did not like vegetable soup, so I served it up as "mulligan stew." We loved sauerkraut and wieners, and if our local merchant was out of wieners, bologna was a good substitute and a delightful surprise to the children. Potatoes cooked with backbone were always welcome. This was before pop was carried out by the carton; kids' appetites were keen, so baked potatoes were relished as much as any dish ever cooked by the chef of the Waldorf Astoria.

Of course, we had our very special dinner for Thanksgiving. From my home, I brought two very cheap but fat hens, and with Mollie's help, we served them a chicken dinner with all the trimmings.

At 12 o'clock, the 14 children found their name cards and were seated on both sides of the table. No queen was ever more gracious at the head of her table than was Mollie at the head of ours. All were seated and we were ready for the blessing.

Jimmie said, "Please bow your heads, while I give thanks." As I listened, I thought, *Jimmie, only you and your Master can know how truly thankful you are.*

With the generous help of a few parents who sent vegetables and meat for stew, we made our money reach through the school year. Each day we could all have all we wanted of one good dish of hot food to supplement the cold lunch of "dist a bistit."

Then came spring and the closing day of school. Fourteen children had been well fed and one schoolteacher made very happy.❖

John Slobodnik

Our New Teacher

By Bessie A. Dean

The bell in the old two-room country schoolhouse called the reluctant pupils from the playground.

It was the first day of school and we had a new teacher. She stood stiffly behind her desk as we entered. She had an uncommonly large nose placed between high cheekbones; her buggy green eyes were slightly slanted and her thin, reddish hair was pulled tightly over a rat which showed in several places. "Rats" were pads that ladies used to arrange their hair around to give it fullness. Her one claim to beauty was her small, well-shaped and manicured hands. We had only to take one look at her to know we had better not try the tricks we had played on the teacher before her.

She waited until we all found our seats and settled down, and then she spoke her first words. "Boys and girls, my name is Miss Margaret Morton. I have been hired by your school board to teach you. I hope to inspire you to absorb all the knowledge you can from your books, but more than that, I hope to help you to become good citizens. The rest is up to you. We will begin by repeating the flag salute, a tribute to this great country of ours."

That first morning was spent with roll call and lesson assignments. Then we were dismissed for a 15-minute recess. Out on the playground, students clustered in little giggly groups, making smart remarks about the new teacher: "… nose like a snowplow … looks like a witch … she would stop a clock …."

We had been told very emphatically the night before to have all our books, pencils and paper with us, and you can bet we did.

These observations came mostly from the boys, but the girls had decided she bought her outmoded clothes at a rummage sale. And they practically had hysterics over the rat in her hair.

School began in earnest the next day. We had been told very emphatically the night before to have all our books, pencils and paper with us—and you can bet we did.

I swear that woman had eyes all around her head. In those days we had double perforated seats in our schoolroom and a favorite trick was to put a pin in the toe of our rubbers and stick it up through the perforation to make the person in front jump. The teacher before Miss Morton had more or less ignored these little pranks, but the first time Sammy Brown, the school clown, tried the pin, he was yanked out of his seat and made to stand in the corner for two whole days.

Another extracurricular activity was hiding behind our geography books and writing notes. I wrote a note to Alice Blakely across the aisle, but as I was delivering it, Miss Morton intercepted and read the note to the whole school. I sat there blushing to the very roots of my hair. To make matters worse, there were many choice remarks in the note about Miss Morton.

I was made to sit on the platform for two whole weeks and denied all recess privileges. Imagine my embarrassment when my smart-aleck schoolmates tittered and pointed at me as they filed outdoors to play. Eventually my sentence was served, but not until she had given me a severe lecture and made me the most ashamed person in the world.

Gradually, we got used to her "master sergeant" tactics and settled down to business. We were not allowed to take anything for granted. Her constant question was "Why?" She insisted that we refer to our dictionaries and encyclopedia when in doubt about a word or if we needed further information on something in our textbooks.

One day in history class, I pronounced the word "corps" as "corpse." Among her other characteristics, she also had a wry sense of humor, and she really made the best of that blooper.

We not only worked our arithmetic problems; we had to prove our answers. That made it impossible to copy the answer from the back of the book.

Autumns in northern Michigan are very beautiful, and one Friday afternoon Miss Morton astonished us by asking how many would like to pack a sack lunch and go on a field trip the next day. We could not believe our ears. Most teachers were so glad to be rid of the kids for two days that they were not about to give up their Saturdays.

A few of the boys did not show up. They may have had farm work to do at home. Even though we were all farmboys and girls and had seen birds, flowers and insects all our lives, what we learned about nature that day absolutely thrilled us. We were having second thoughts about Miss Morton. She was becoming better looking all the time.

We had one little country church that was served by a minister from a nearby town. He drove out on Sunday afternoons to our church. Who do you think was the soloist in the choir? It was Miss Morton, and she had the most beautiful, clear soprano voice I had ever heard.

Miss Morton had the most beautiful, clear soprano voice I had ever heard.

Day by day, our school settled into a well-organized plan. Not only were we taught the three Rs, we were taught to appreciate good books and works of art, some copies of which she had purchased with proceeds from a box social. We learned the proper way to read and enjoy poetry.

One day our teacher read *The Bells* by Edgar Allan Poe, and we could almost hear the bells ringing as she read. We memorized a great deal of poetry in those days, and some of the beautiful passages from *Evangeline* and *Hiawatha* will stay in my memory always. We learned Portia's mercy speech from *The Merchant of Venice*, and many more gems from literature. She also found many opportunities to show us some of the social graces.

Little by little, Miss Morton made herself a very vital and respected part of our little community. She taught a Sunday school class and had organized a group of young adults for book reviews and Bible study. During the winter months, she and some of the other grown-ups were our chaperones for sleigh rides, movie outings, or for trips to some home to play games, sing and pop corn.

She taught at our school for three years and they passed quickly. At that time, all country school eighth graders had to take a state examination before entering high school. Our school had the highest grades in the county.

When we had our graduating exercise and had to bid our teacher goodbye, we were very sad. She, too, left that year to go back to college to work on her degree.

As we all gathered at the depot the day she left, we waved a tearful goodbye and agreed that with all that inner beauty, she did not need physical beauty. But we no longer noticed her plain features. Of all the teachers I have ever had, she is the one I remember most vividly. Her wisdom and dedication have helped guide me all these years. ❖

Grammar in Rhyme

Three little words you often see
Are Articles—a, an, and the;
A Noun is the name of anything,
As school or garden, hoop or swing.

Adjectives tell the kind of Noun,
As great, small, pretty, white or brown.
Instead of Nouns, the Pronouns stand—
Her head, his face, your arm, my hand.

Verbs tell of something to be done:
To bear, count, sing, laugh, study, run.
How things are done, the Adverbs tell,
As slowly, quickly, ill, or well.

Conjunctions join the words together,
As man and woman, wind or weather.
The Prepositions stand before
A Noun, as of or through a door.

The Interjections shows surprise,
As, ah! how pretty! oh! how wise!
The whole are called Nine Parts of Speech
Which reading, writing, speaking teach.

Unknown

Yuletides, Halloweens and Other Special Days

Chapter Three

*W*here is he that is born King of the Jews? For we have seen his star in the East, and are come to worship him." Those were the only words I had to memorize for the school's Christmas pageant. Twenty-five simple words from the Gospel according to St. Matthew.

All I had to do was lead two other kings of the East up to "Herod" and say those 25 words. Then it was off to the manger with gold, frankincense and myrrh—our gifts for the newborn King.

I knew how important it was to get it right— Mrs. Drake, the director and my third-grade teacher, had emphasized that to all of us elementary students who were saddled with speaking parts. All our parents would be there, along with a lot of really important people like school board members and county officials.

Just 25 simple words. I could do that.

"Where is he that is born King of the Jews?" I queried Mama over the dinner dishes (she washed, I dried).

"Wha ...? ... Oh, your lines for the pageant," Mama said. She always was pretty quick on such things.

"... For we saw his star in the East ..."

"You mean, 'For we have *seen* his star in the East ... ' " She also was pretty quick to catch and correct 8-year-old mistakes.

"Oh, shoot. ... For we have *seen* his star in the East, and are come to worship him." Mama smiled and nodded. Dishes were clean and so was my delivery.

The next few days were spent addressing every critter on the farm, every fence post, every person who dared show his or her face with the same query: "Where is he that is born King of the Jews? ..."

By Friday, the last day of school before Christmas break, I had the lines down perfectly.

The night of the pageant was suddenly upon us. The event was scheduled for the local nondenominational church which at least had a small raised platform to serve as a stage. In the adjacent Sunday school rooms, several nervous children gathered to put on primitive costumes and make final preparations.

"Where is he that is born King of the Jews?" I asked "Joseph," a fourth-grader.

"Shut up!" was his only response.

Finally we were ready. The Christ child was in the manger, surrounded by angels and shepherds. We three kings came to Herod, and I intoned my lines perfectly. In the crowd, Mama and Daddy smiled proudly. Off to stage-right, Mrs. Drake moved on to worrying about the next child's lines. In the front row, the important people didn't even notice the relief on my 8-year-old face. In Jerusalem, we hastily moved on toward Bethlehem.

All the week's fretting and it was over in a matter of a few seconds.

What was not over in a few seconds, however, was the memory. That memory and many more like it were what made holidays in little country schoolhouses back then so special. Yuletides, Halloweens and other special days were some of the best times of the Good Old Days.

—*Ken Tate*

Halloween Party

By Virginia Hearn Machir

I remember the high-school Halloween party when I was a sophomore at Winfield High School in Missouri. Our teacher told us there would be three prizes awarded for costumes—prettiest costume, best disguise, and another for a booby prize. There would also be games and refreshments.

The sophomore girls were all agog, planning their costumes, but no one told anyone except her best friend what her costume was going to be—and she was sworn to secrecy. In those days there was no "trick or treat," or store-bought costumes. Most of the students at Winfield High made their own.

I decided I was going to try for prettiest costume. My mother was very adept with the needle and she made me a costume from orange and black crepe paper, sewn onto the foundation of a white cotton slip. I thought it was beautiful, with black straps across the shoulders, and an orange bodice with rows of full, gathered ruffles from the waist down. With this I wore a black harlequin eye mask, big orange earrings and black patent leather slippers with Cuban heels. I felt beautiful in my costume and told my best friend, Tiny, that it represented the spirit of Halloween.

The decorating committee decorated the basement with dried stalks and shocks of corn and huge orange jack-o'-lanterns.

The decorating committee decorated the basement with dried stalks and shocks of corn and huge orange jack-o'-lanterns. Orange and black streamers of crepe paper were draped from corner to corner of the ceiling. Black cats and witches flying on brooms were cut from construction paper and attached to the walls.

Finally, the night of the Halloween party arrived. I had a date with a boy named Jack and he brought his younger brother, Bob, and his date along. Jack drove a Model-A Ford coupe, a "one-seater." Bob wanted to drive his big brother's car, so I was forced to sit on Jack's lap. I feared my crepe paper costume would be wrinkled by the time we reached the high school.

When we arrived at the Halloween party, I inspected my costume before we went in. I decided it hadn't gotten too wrinkled, even though we had been crowded into the one-seater coupe.

As we entered the basement, the hubbub of happy laughter and voices filled our ears. I looked around and did not recognize any of my classmates. There were witches in black, ghosts in white, and gypsies wearing bright, colored skirts and blouses, with dozens of colorful beads around their necks and scarves tied over their heads. There were cowboys and Indians and hoboes. There was much guessing of who was who behind the Halloween masks. Some students never were guessed because they refused to talk and be recognized by their voices.

One corner of the basement had been curtained off and transformed into a haunted house. Screeches and yells and weird noises came from the haunted house as classmates were "frightened" by the skeletons and witches lurking in dark places.

We bobbed for apples, and then there was the grand march for costume judging. Everyone marched around in a circle. Three teachers were judges. They would take the hand of one of the marchers and withdraw him from the competition. One by one the marchers were pulled from the circle until there were only three other contestants besides me. My heart was beating a mile a minute for I knew there were only three prizes to be given. Just then, one of the teachers grasped my arm and removed me from the circle! What a horrendous disappointment!

The girl who beat me out was dressed as Jean Harlow, with a pretty platinum-blond wig; long, slinky blue dress; and a pretty girl's mask. She had a picture of Jean Harlow pinned on her back and she won the prize for the prettiest costume. A boy dressed as a fat woman won the prize for the best disguise. He had refused to talk to anyone all night and no one had been able to guess his identity. A boy in a clown suit, who had entertained the crowd with handsprings and comical antics, won the booby prize. Of course, I was disappointed, but I consoled myself with the thought that I had been in the running.

The refreshment committee had done themselves proud. There was delicious, hot, spiced apple cider, as well as plates heaped high with sugary doughnuts and pumpkin pie. We removed our masks and stuffed our faces as only teenagers can do. Then it was time to go and we bid adieu to our classmates. Everyone agreed it had been a wonderful party.

We started for home in the one-seater Model-A coupe, Bob driving, his date sitting in the middle, with Jack next to her and me sitting on Jack's lap. At that time Highway 79 through Winfield was a gravel road. We had just crossed

There were witches in black, ghosts in white, and gypsies wearing bright, colored skirts and blouses.

a small bridge north of Winfield, and all of us were laughing hilariously over some incident at the party, when Bob suddenly lost control of the car. The next thing we knew we were in the loose gravel on the shoulder of the highway. Then the car rolled over the 10-foot embankment and landed on its top at the bottom of the ditch. I could hear the tinkle of broken glass and the gurgle of water, or gasoline, running out of the car.

"Is anybody hurt?" Jack yelled. No one seemed to be; we had been going very slowly.

"Turn off the motor," Jack told Bob. He turned off the motor; we opened the doors and climbed out of the upside-down automobile as best we could and stood on the shoulder of the highway, a very subdued and frightened group. Bob had a cut on his forehead, but it wasn't serious. Then I discovered the crepe-paper ruffles on my Halloween costume had torn. One of the ruffles was hanging down to my ankles.

"Thank God nobody is hurt," Jack said.

About that time, a car came along the highway and stopped. It was a man from Foley who knew all of us and he agreed to take us home, all except Jack, who stayed to look after his car and try to get it towed to a garage.

When I got home I woke Father and Mother to tell them about the accident.

"No, nobody was hurt," I assured them.

Then father began to laugh. "Just look at our Halloween Spirit now!" he said. I looked down at my crepe-paper costume. A three-cornered tear in the orange crepe-paper bodice left a large expanse of white cotton slip exposed. The gathered paper ruffles had come ungathered in spots. Besides the one ruffle that hung to my ankles, the others hung in ragged disarray. There was a big hole in the knee of my hose where my knee had been cut. Then I discovered I had lost one of my earrings.

"Oh, I lost one of my earrings," I said stupidly.

"Well, you can be thankful you didn't lose one of your legs," Father said.

If I live to be 100 I will never forget my crepe-paper costume and that night of my high-school Halloween party. ❖

School Programs

By Myrna Morlan

Remember the school programs that were put on in the one-room schoolhouse? For weeks before, you and your classmates rehearsed—at recess and after school, because studies had to go on as usual during school time. Each one had his or her part, from the littlest one on up. There were recitations and one-act plays.

A stage was built right into one end of the old schoolroom. With the help of the older boys, the teacher strung a wire across in front of this stage and hung the curtain that seemed to be part of the old school's furnishings. Another curtain was hung at each end, to make a dressing room for the boys and another for the girls. Different students were assigned the chore of pulling the curtain open on opening night, and what a thrill that was!

The old potbellied stove seemed to eat up the coal almost as fast as we kids could carry it in by the bucketful from the coal shed out back. A big round jacket stood around the stove so no one could burn himself, and on really cold days, the teacher would let us sit around it in campfire fashion and put our feet on the jacket to keep us warm.

Everyone worked like mad to polish up their recitations, but I suspect no one worked as hard as that poor teacher.

Notes were sent home to the parents to let everyone know the night of the big program and to tell the mothers what to bring for the lunch afterward.

Everyone worked like mad to polish up their recitations, but I suspect no one worked as hard as that poor teacher who also had to keep eight grades going besides producing a polished performance.

The night of the program was exciting. We were washed and scrubbed; our hair combed just so. Usually we wore new or nearly new clothes. Every mama and papa had to see their little darlings perform their solo recitations. Then, there were one-act plays and sometimes some short three-act ones. There were costumes to don, and such a snickering and shushing going on in each dressing room as the teacher raced from one end of the stage to the other. It was always a great temptation to sneak a peek out front to see the audience. But oh, how scared we were, right down in the pits of our stomachs, when we saw all those faces looking at us! Then we were sure we wouldn't remember one word of our parts.

A girl in my class and I were given parts for a singing act. We worked so hard at it that it rings in my head yet. I was small for my age so I was given the girl part, and she was dressed as the boy. (We wouldn't have wanted a *boy* playing the boy's part; we were too bashful!)

When the curtains opened, there I was, sitting on a small sofa in my long dress. When a knock came on the door, I went to the door and the singing began:

Me: "Good evening, Zachariah."
She: "And howdy, Mary Jane."
Me: "It's awful nice this evening."
She: "Excepting for the rain."
We: "But we'll be warm and comfy, a-sitting here tonight,
Without a fire or lamplight, for love is burning bright."

Then came the chorus:

"Oh, gee, but ain't it jolly, a-sparking, you and me,

I bet some folks are jealous—um-huh, I bet they be,
And older folks are wishing
That they were young again
To court their Zachariah—and kiss their Mary Jane!"

There were more verses, and at the end of each chorus we moved closer to one another as the crowd snickered. At the end, we were sitting very close with our heads together.

And then it was all over. The clapping began, the teacher thanked the audience and, oh, what a relief it was! But again, I suspect it was the poor teacher who was most relieved.

Then the fun began as the ladies cut the pies and started the coffee. The men visited while the kids ran in every direction. Oh, how good those pies were! And no one seemed to worry about eating more than one piece and ruining his or her diet. It was all one big, happy time. Remember? ❖

Open House Blues

By Alan Sanderson

pen-house blues—that's the only way I can describe these annual meetings of parents and teachers with me sandwiched in between. I had to put up with such ordeals through nine years of learning, and not one of them rated a definite plus for me. Naturally, some were less tolerable than others, but since these make the more interesting reading, these are what I shall dwell upon.

Although open house was regularly scheduled for the beginning of November, preparations actually began with the start of classes immediately following the Labor Day weekend—that is, assuming a pupil had learned to paste, wield a crayon and draw a reasonably straight line with the aid of a ruler. Accomplishments of this caliber entitled every luckless boy and girl to make a folder in which would be placed all other demeaning scraps of schoolwork.

Under the sour supervision of our visiting art teacher who came in once a week, we learned how to glue two large sheets of stiff, white drawing paper to a common binder. Next, we were taught how to create an "original" design that was to be repeated eight times on the outer covers. Next came the neat lettering of our individual names in the upper right-hand corner. Perhaps the fact that I normally added this finishing touch sometime after the Thanksgiving holidays guaranteed me at least a rocky approach to this get-together.

We rehearsed so much that my well-worn lines became a source of irritation to me.

Fourth-grade festivities presented me with an opportunity to gain a measure of inner satisfaction. Having a part in a class play was infinitely better than merely attending these functions with an air of resignation. For some reason known only to our teacher, our efforts dealt with an episode in the life of Abraham Lincoln. We rehearsed so much that my well-worn lines extolling the famed honesty of our 16th president became a source of irritation to me, but because my dad planned on being there this time, too, I voiced no complaint. My final delivery promised to be a moment I wouldn't forget, and it was, though not in the mold I'd visualized. Somehow I muffed the remark I could say unerringly in my sleep. Instead of uttering, "Abe would walk seven miles to repay a penny," it embarrassingly came out, "Abe would walk seven pennies to repay a mile." My quick correction only prompted a ripple of good-natured laughter. I was mortified!

Two years later, a different kind of open house project was unveiled. Due to my profound liking for history and geography, I was commissioned to draw a map of the world on the blackboard at the back of the room. Being able to use all sorts of colored chalk excited me. A second fringe benefit surfaced when I was informed that I could work on this assignment during our lessons. Too many jarring squeaks from my chalk almost killed this privilege (and my blossoming creation, to boot) more than once.

In the end, I rather wished it had, because my finished product in no manner resembled anything on this planet, not when some projection labeled India nearly touched the South Pole. I pleaded with my teacher for permission to erase the whole mess. My request was denied. There simply wasn't time to come up with a substitute display. My lone saving grace was "forgetting" to sign my name to that monstrosity, thereby keeping most of the visiting adults in the dark as to who was responsible.

The open house conducted by the school's graduating class was always something special. It had to be, since eighth graders were supposed to set marks of achievement worthy of imitation by the young children. They couldn't be fooled, either. After the big night, the departing group had the additional privilege of showing the other seven grades what they had concocted.

For us, there could be only one choice: We'd put on a "radio show." Earlier in the year we'd taken a trip to the Outlet Company in Providence, R.I., where we'd been the guests of WJAR as it aired live the music of Earl Shean and his orchestra. Our view couldn't have been better. The entire class sat in a row of portable chairs stretching from one end of the stage to the other, and facing the band. I can still hear the announcer telling us that while it would be appreciated if quiet could be maintained, we didn't have to impersonate

A warm feeling of pride pulsated through me as I tried to conjure up the honeyed phrases with which my teacher would fill her ears.

robots. Commercials included, it was an exhilarating experience for a 12-year-old.

From that point on, the question wasn't what we should do, but how. The largest problem was duplicating the wonderful gadgetry of the control room. After several discussions, we agreed on a cardboard stand decorated with imaginary colored lights and dials which would be suspended in the left front corner. Here, a boy would sit with his back temporarily to the class. After some make-believe knob twisting, he was to suddenly whirl about and point to our "announcer," who was standing in the center before a realistic microphone someone had fashioned out of old piping. This professional gesture signaled that the announcer was now "on the air." Of course, we couldn't assemble a proper band, but a singing quartet was introduced to the audience, supported by fine piano accompaniment. On this supreme occasion, I didn't make a single blunder; much to my disappointment, I evidently wasn't trusted well enough to land a role.

Promotion to a big city high school offered no escape—at least for my freshman year. Still, I didn't think anything could go wrong there. Frills were a bane of the past. Folders, plays and recitals weren't part of the new scene. Also, to my surprise, the marks I'd received for that all-important first quarter had been better than I'd expected, and I found myself getting along quite well with my teachers. I figured it would just be a friendly chat amongst everyone concerned. Maybe one or two scholastic compliments would even be tossed in my direction.

The evening started pleasantly enough. My mom and I took an early bus and I had an hour to show her around this spacious new school of mine. She was visibly impressed by the number of classrooms (my previous alma mater held only eight, which would barely accommodate just the first-year students at my

new level), the gleaming corridors and the proportions of the auditorium. A warm feeling of pride pulsated through me as I tried to conjure up the honeyed phrases with which my teacher would fill her ears.

He was deeply engrossed in conversation when we entered my homeroom. To fill in our wait, I showed my mom the desk at which I toiled and let her leaf through some of my luckier test papers. Presently, I snatched my chance and led her to my instructor where I faultlessly provided the introductions. The smug smile I wore must've vanished more quickly than a cookie after a week's fast. My mom was thrown for a verbal loss by his opening question. Very courteously he asked why she'd come. The ones he really thought it important to meet were the parents of pupils in educational trouble. We left shortly afterward.

My mom didn't come again. Neither did I. That in itself, I suppose, could constitute a happy ending to my open-house blues. ❖

Box Socials

By Delores Smith

I wonder how many people remember the box socials at the little country schools? I attended grade school in a small Indiana town, where I proudly graduated from the eighth grade in 1933. I went on to other schools for the higher grades.

When I started in the first grade, our schoolhouse was a small, two-room brick building, and included all eight grades of grammar school. A few years later, an addition had to be made due to the increased number of pupils. Two more rooms with their own potbellied stoves (that was our only source of heat at the time) were constructed in the basement of the old schoolhouse.

Oh, what a day of celebration that was! Now the rooms held only two grades apiece! I'm sure it was a relief for the two original teachers, in more ways than one.

As I remember, our box socials were held on the last Friday evening of every month—at least that's the way it was at the Broadview School in Monroe County, Ind.

A week or so before the happy occasion, the girl pupils, with much help from their families, busily searched for original ideas as to how to decorate a box. It was usually a shoebox that had held a pair of shoes ordered from Sears Roebuck. To decorate it, they used crepe paper, bows, ribbons, beads … anything colorful and fancy they could find around the house.

When that eventful Friday finally arrived, Mother helped pack the beautiful box with food for two—cold snacks, hard-boiled eggs, cakes, pickles and so forth.

The girl pupils, with much help from their families, busily searched for original ideas as to how to decorate a box.

That evening everybody gathered at the schoolhouse, parents included. It seems like in those days parents shared everything with their children.

The boxes packed with goodies were then put up for auction to the highest bidder. The proceeds were used to purchase whatever playground equipment was needed.

We girls, who always seemed to have a very special young man friend in mind, somehow managed to let him know how we had decorated our own boxes, so he would know which one to bid on.

Oh, what a joy when our young friend won our box, and we could enjoy that wonderful snack together in some dimly lit spot where we thought we were all alone! ❖

Thanksgiving Dinner

By Rhoda Woods

As most of our older readers will remember, our country schools were run by school directors who had the power to say "yes" or "no" to just about anything concerning the school. Having been born and raised on a farm, I came under their jurisdiction when I was in school, and to this day, I have nothing but good to say for the old country schools.

However, back about 1919, our directors said, "No" to Thanksgiving Day off. I don't know why; it was probably a makeup day. Of course, this day was a big occasion in our family of eight, and we were all crushed, but my dear parents came to the rescue. Mom said Dad would bring our lunches to school on the hayrack while he was on his way to the neighbor's for a load of hay.

Immediately after we left for school that morning (without our dinner buckets), Mom and Dad got busy. They prepared six pigeons the same as you would a turkey. If you've never seen a roast pigeon, it looks just like a miniature turkey, full-breasted and all. With these they brought dressing, mashed potatoes and gravy, homemade sweet pickles and a whole pumpkin pie, cut in six pieces.

They packed helpings in saucers, old-fashioned coffee mugs and whatever else Mom could round up.

They packed individual helpings in saucers, old-fashioned coffee mugs and whatever else Mom could round up. It was all packed in one of those large, black, bread pans with another one over the top, and then covered with a blanket. (I can't recall how we got that rigmarole home, but Mom continued to bake huge pans of bread, so we must have gotten them back to her kitchen somehow.)

We partook of this sumptuous Thanksgiving dinner while the other kids were choking down soggy bread-and-jelly sandwiches and boiled eggs.

So, that Thanksgiving dinner at school ended up as one of the most memorable we ever had. Through it we affirmed one very important fact—we six children had the best dad and mom in the whole world. ❖

A Very Special Tree

By Mildred Goff

There were 14 unhappy faces in that one-room schoolhouse in Iowa many years ago.

"But, Teacher, it won't seem like Christmas if we can't have a tree," one of the girls said.

"I know. I'm sorry," Teacher told her. "But no one has offered us a tree this year. I don't know where we can get one. Do you?"

We didn't. In those days, there were no trees for sale in the stores. None of us would have a Christmas tree at home. We hung up stockings and Santa filled them with candy and popcorn balls and oranges, but the Christmas party at the schoolhouse, and the tree, made the real celebration for us.

"We might as well not have our party if we can't have a tree." She was looking out a window and we looked too, but there was nothing to be seen but a row of bare willow trees, plowed fields and low, gray clouds.

Suddenly Teacher looked back at us, her eyes shining. "John, " she said, "doesn't that field next to us belong to your father?" John nodded. "Do you suppose he would let us have that old crab apple tree in the corner?"

"I know he would," John said. "It has to come out of there. He told me to cut it down, but I didn't do it yet."

"Well, then," Teacher said briskly, "there's our tree. Get the hatchet, John, and you and Bill go cut the tree and bring it here. The rest of us will look for things we can use to decorate with."

We went out into the chilly air, grumbling and complaining. "It doesn't seem a bit like Christmas. It isn't even snowing. No snow. No tree. Shucks!"

Teacher brought out a big can of popcorn, and we made long popcorn strings to loop on the branches, white on white.

While the big boys cut down the tree and dragged it to the schoolhouse, the rest of us hunted along the road banks. We found long, trailing branches of bittersweet with bright berries like little orange lanterns. We gathered milkweed pods, tall, brown cattails and feathery plumes of dried grass. We took our finds back to the schoolhouse, and there the thorny tree stood near Teacher's desk, looking very much out of place.

"I'll have a fine surprise for you tomorrow," Teacher promised. "We are going to have a beautiful Christmas tree. Just you wait and see."

We cheered up a little. Teacher was smart; we knew that. We didn't know what she could do about that ugly old tree, but we trusted her.

The next morning, everyone was at school very early, wondering about the mysterious packages on Teacher's desk, but she did not open them. She set us to work. The girls washed the windows, and the boys polished the stove and swept the pine floor. We cleaned the blackboards, and I was given the envied task of clapping the erasers together outdoors to get the chalk dust out of them. We hung red and green paper chains at the windows, and looped them from the ceiling. Teacher wrote "Merry Christmas" on the blackboard with red and green chalk, and drew a fancy border of holly leaves and berries. The room looked very festive now, except for that awful old tree.

We crowded around her desk while Teacher opened one of the big bundles. Everyone was disappointed; it was just plain, white cotton batting. Our mothers used it to line quilts. We couldn't do anything with that!

Teacher tore off a long strip of the white cotton and wrapped it around one of the black, thorny branches. "We are going to turn this into a beautiful, white Christmas tree," she said. "Come on now, get busy. Everyone must help."

We had to obey, so we began winding the white cotton around the awkward branches. The thorns stuck our fingers. The cotton made us sneeze. We felt cheated and cross.

I went to the back of the room to get a drink from the water bucket setting on a bench, and turned around to look at the tree. It was changing. Where the black branches were covered with white, it looked very different—almost pretty.

At last, every twig was covered. Teacher brought out a big can of popcorn, and we made long popcorn strings to loop on the branches, white on white. Tiny white candles were clipped on the tips of the twigs, and at the very top perched a glittering white angel.

We began to feel quite proud and excited. Anyone, we told each other, could have a plain old evergreen, but our tree was something special. We stood admiring it for a moment, and then Teacher pulled red curtains across the end of the room to hide it away.

"Time to go home now," she said. "Hurry back."

That evening, in the early dark, the neighborhood converged on the hollow where the schoolhouse sat, lights shining from its windows into the lightly falling snow. Inside, grown-ups and children sat at every desk and bench, talking and laughing, noisy as a tree full of blackbirds. The tree was hidden behind the red curtains. Teacher stepped to the front of the room, and our program began. We recited and sang, and our parents applauded everything. Then everyone sang *Jingle Bells*, and we all applauded ourselves. At last, Teacher threw open the curtains at the end of the room. There stood our white tree.

Everyone was silent for a moment. We children looked at each other, worried and anxious. What would people think of it? To me, it looked beautiful, as white and delicate as a snowflake.

Then everyone began to applaud. "That's the prettiest Christmas tree I ever saw!" someone said.

I thought so, too, and many years later, I still do. ❖

John Slobodnik

Rural School Christmas

By Ivanelle Ruetten

Oh, how happy I am that I attended a rural school, especially when I remember our wonderful Christmas programs. We started before Thanksgiving, selecting the plays, recitations and songs to be performed. This preparation was as much fun as the program itself! We strung red and green crepe-paper streamers across the ceiling and hung bells. We put up a long wire across the front of our "stage" from one side of the school to the other. On it, we hung curtains to cover the whole stage; they were drawn before and after each scene so we could set up the props for the following play.

I was blessed with a very talented mother who created many of these plays and songs. I especially remember one called *Grandma's Lost Teeth* or *What's the Matter, Grandma?* For it, I had to make a pair of false teeth. Thanks again to my mother's generosity, I was able to use hers for a model, and I molded a pair out of paraffin! I made two gum foundations and colored them with rose-colored nail polish. I'm sure I thought I was as good as dentist when I formed each tooth and fastened it to each gum. When we were through with them after the program, I gave them to my friend "Zip" Zifka. Being toothless and endowed with a great sense of humor, he had many hours of fun entertaining his friends at the corner pub!

A Christmas program was not complete without a Christmas tree. Not wanting to leave anyone out, our teacher let us all go to Pine Knob to select and cut our own tree. You can't believe how well we completed our

Not wanting to leave anyone out, our teacher let us all go to Pine Knob to select and cut our own tree.

schoolwork so that we might all enjoy the trip. After careful scrutiny, we selected our favorite tree, and with the help of the big eighth-grade boys, we cut it and pulled it home on the sled. When it was placed in the corner of the room and decorated, the magic of Christmas had begun!

We each drew names and kept secret whose name we had drawn. We bought a gift for that person. The teacher received a gift from each family.

While the last plays were being performed and Silent Night was being sung, someone would slip out the door unnoticed and dress in Santa's outfit. When the room was silent, the sleigh bells rang and Santa arrived!

Oh, to see the eyes of the youngest children as they climbed in fear and delight on their mothers' laps! There was a bag of candy for every child and a red delicious apple for all. The pupils opened their gifts as their names were called, and showed off their presents to their parents—pencil boxes, necklaces or what have you. The teacher also gave a gift to each pupil.

Riding home in the sleigh filled with clean, fresh straw, we snuggled down under the horse blanket as the horses puffed their "steam" into the cold air. Oh, how happy we were! Vacation was coming up, and best of all, Christmas was coming, too!

I am so grateful that I had the opportunity to attend a rural school. Perhaps my little saga about one of my happiest moments there will give someone else a chance to share my joy. I hope so! ❖

Christmas Dinner

By Pearl Hynes MacEachern

Way back in 1916, when I was a little girl, 11 years old, my father bought some lots in a new subdivision of Elmira Heights just outside the village that were to become known as the Wilbur Plot.

Just why it was called that, I never did understand. I do know it was a poor man's paradise since there were no restrictions on buildings. Large families could live in two- and three-room houses that were built out of anything on hand and then added onto and covered over later. Others built nicer houses. But *all* the children went to Lenox Avenue School, District No. 5, and what a school that was!

Each child was given a piece to speak, or a part in a little play, or some little drill, and all the parents were invited to come.

I was the oldest child in our family, with two younger brothers. My youngest brother started school there. I attended the fifth grade there and finished the seventh and half of the eighth there.

Our teacher, Mrs. Van Deusen, was an elderly lady who had taught school in that district and raised her own family. Her husband was an ocean-going captain.

Lenox Avenue School was considered the "new" school at that time. It had only two rooms. The old school, over the Erie-Pennsylvania Railroad, was called "the old brick school."

With the influx of new families, the new school soon filled up. In those days, we didn't have baseball, basketball or any such things like we do now, but Mrs. Van Deusen sure taught us a lot more than the three R's.

But to get back to Christmas dinner, every year each child who could draw anything at all was encouraged to do so. The teacher bought art paper or art boards, often at her own expense, so the artwork would be special.

We mounted things like leaves, twigs, bugs, butterflies and moths. Teacher always saved them all, and each year at fair time, she would mount our displays on poster board and enter them in the Chamung County Fair. Our school always got good money for prizes.

We children were allowed to vote on how this money was to be spent (some sports equipment, books for the library, etc.), but teacher always set aside a portion of it for Christmas. At Christmastime, we exchanged names for a gift not to cost more than 10 cents.

Ten cents in those days bought quite a lot. *The Star Gazette*, the daily paper, was 10 cents per week. I know, because I had a paper route.

Each child was given a piece to speak, or a part in a little play, or some little drill, and all the parents were invited to come on the afternoon of the last day of school before Christmas vacation.

With the rest of the fair money, Mrs. Van Deusen bought a huge piece of beef, which she roasted herself; potatoes, usually more than a bushel, which she peeled herself; and some kind of vegetable. She would have some of the mothers cook the potatoes and mash them, then bring them to the school when they came.

Some mothers made Jell-O and some made cake, and after all the entertainment was over, each child had a Christmas dinner. You just can't imagine what fun it was. For many of those children, I am sure that was all the Christmas dinner they had.

I will never forget those dinners and times, and I'll bet there are a lot of others who won't, either. ❖

All-Night Christmas Party

By Mary Hilbert

t was subzero weather and threatening snow on the night of the annual school party in December 1930. My mother checked with some of the neighbors via the 10-party rural phone to make sure everyone still planned to go. We children held our breaths. *Not go to the Christmas party!* It was unthinkable. The 15 children in our one-room schoolhouse had practiced their parts for this special program for months and months, and the excitement had built up to the usual fever pitch.

Everyone had a part to play, regardless of his or her proclivity for the performing arts. In fact, occasionally a reluctant few had to be dragged, kicking and screaming, onto the stage—sometimes with hilarious results. Perform we must, because our parents expected it. The real hams were given leading roles, or performed solos.

One year, the teacher tried to teach us to sing in harmony—a challenge, considering scarcely half a dozen of us could carry a tune. A Fred Waring chorus we were not. Nevertheless, she plunged on and the resulting applause rocked the rafters as the audience attempted to mask their explosive laughter! My mother tells me it was a riot.

Although horses are famous for finding their way home in a blizzard, it was deemed too dangerous to start out.

No, we couldn't possibly miss the Christmas program. The mothers always made tons of sandwiches, salads, pies, cakes and homemade ice cream. No problem keeping the ice cream cold! In fact, *all* the refreshments were often frozen by the time they arrived at the schoolhouse.

But my father was really worried this year; he could almost forecast the weather in his bones. However, everyone else was going, so he hitched old Maggie and Rob to the bobsled and we packed up. This sled had a wagon frame on a single runner; pipes on the sides held up a canvas that protected us from the elements. The floor of the sleigh was filled with straw for insulation, and we wrapped ourselves in fur robes. There was a small barn with plenty of hay for the horses at the school, which was about two miles away across the bleak prairie.

By the time we arrived, the wind had risen ominously, and the person in charge of stoking up the coal furnace had arrived late, so it was barely warmer inside than it was out. We performed that year with jackets, mittens and chattering teeth, but it didn't dampen our enthusiasm a bit. Santa managed to arrive on time (weather, we knew, would never detain Santa) to hand out the precious apples, oranges and candy canes.

By the time lunch was over, a howling blizzard was attacking the little schoolhouse with full-blown fury. Although horses are famous for finding their way home in a blizzard, it was deemed too dangerous to start out. The prospect of sleeping all night in the school was tremendously exciting to us kids. All of the fur robes and blankets were brought in and makeshift beds were made up on the cold floor, accompanied by much hilarity.

There was a great deal of giggling discussion and argument as to who was going to sleep next to whom, the exact proximity to

one's neighbor or friend, and how far away the boys and girls should be. Crucial decisions like these took up a good share of the night, but we were eventually bedded down and managed to drop off to sleep sometime before morning.

It was no picnic for the parents who had to make themselves as comfortable as possible, keeping one eye on the furnace and one on the weather.

By morning, the worst of the storm had passed, and after a cold breakfast of sandwiches and cake, the weary parents took us home.

"That sure was a fun Christmas," my little brother murmured sleepily as we huddled together in the sleigh.

"It sure was," my older brother and I agreed. Mother and Daddy were strangely silent.❖

To My Valentine With Love

By Lois Kullberg

Hi, Mom," greeted my 6-ear-old daughter, Karen, as she came home from school. "I have to have 32 valentines by next Tuesday," she informed me while holding up a neatly copied list of names.

"Why do you need 32 cards?" I asked.

"Because we have 32 kids in our class," she replied matter-of-factly.

"Do you have to send a card to every child in the room?"

"Oh, yes, everyone does." Concluding the discussion, she picked up her jump rope and ran outdoors.

Then my second-grader, Mark, told me that last year his teacher hung up large, brown paper bags with each child's name on one. The children dropped their cards in the sacks as they brought them to school during the week before Valentine's Day. That way the sorting was done automatically, instead of being delivered by a "postman," as we did it in the "old days." Things had certainly changed! During my grade-school days, popularity was measured by the number of valentines a person received. When I was in the sixth grade, I got more valentines than any other kid in my room. What a feeling of triumph! When kids gave cards because they wanted to, rather than necessity, it made a person feel like they had earned them.

Another important part of Valentine's Day when I was in grade school was the valentine box.

Another important part of Valentine's Day when I was in grade school was the valentine box. It was a glorious creation of red and white crepe paper ruffles, lacy white doilies, and red construction-paper hearts. If it was real fancy, it even had gold cupids on it.

We had a box like that once. A girl named Sandra and I were appointed to make the valentine box. For three weeks she kept finding excuses for not working on it with me. The kids kept asking when we were going to bring the box to school. Finally, in desperation, with just a week left until Valentine's Day, I decided to make the box myself.

The corner store was out of red, pink and white crepe paper, so I had to settle for aqua, which did not please me at all. I pasted the crepe paper neatly around the sides of the box and ruffled the edges by stretching the paper. I covered the top of the box with white typing paper and liberally covered the box with hearts—big, small, skinny and fat. I didn't like aqua on a valentine box, but at least I hadn't let the kids down.

Monday morning I set the box on the teacher's front table. A few of the kids had valentines to put in it. They made comments like, "How come it's blue?" "I see you finally got it here." "Mrs. Taylor's room had theirs all last week."

Just then Sandra arrived. I wanted to sink through the floor. Her mother had made a beautiful valentine box for her. The sides were covered with red crepe-paper pleats that she had sewn together on her sewing machine. Next, she made yards and yards of frothy white ruffles. They were placed on top of the box and looked like frosting on a cake. A lacy heart decorated the front of the box.

Nobody even looked at my plain little aqua valentine box after that. One girl, who came in late, said in a loud voice, "I'm going to put my cards in the pretty box." Another child from the room across the hall asked why we had that "old blue box."

My feelings were crushed! I ran to the girls' bathroom and cried. Nobody had appreciated my efforts!

After class, I lingered until everyone had left the room. Then I reached into my "old blue box," took out the few cards inside, and put them in Sandra's box. I picked up my box and started home. On my way, I had to stop by the kindergarten room to pick up my little sister.

"Where are you going with that pretty valentine box?" asked my sister's teacher.

"I'm taking it home because the kids don't like it," I answered. Then came the whole story.

She asked me if she could have the box for her room. She really thought it was pretty. Gratefully, I handed the box to her. I could have kissed her! Come to think of it, that was the same year I won the "popularity contest" for having the most valentines. Do you suppose she might have had something to do with it?

Another difference is that today's younger generation interprets the messages on the cards. I never paid much attention if a card said something like "You are my ideal"; it was just a card. While watching Karen and Mark address their cards, I realized words mean more than they used to. It was all I could do to keep from laughing as I overheard their conversation.

"Oh, boy, this one will really kill Tammy," said Mark, as he cut out a heart with the picture of a girl on it. The card said, "You are my ideal."

"Either it will kill her, or she'll kill you," commented Karen.

"Hee, hee, hee," she giggled a minute later. "Look at this stamp I'm putting on the back of Jeff's envelope: 'Twenty Kisses, Twenty Hugs.'"

Well, I guess it can be said that the younger generation is more sincere anyway!

Come to think of it, I recall some comic valentines that we hoped would put a message across, too. They were perfectly awful. During the late '40s, we had comic valentines printed on a single sheet. They folded into thirds instead of coming with an envelope. There were pictures of ugly bosses, teachers and monster animals, among other things. You could send someone you didn't particularly like a comic valentine without signing your name—to sort of get even. As your school "postman" handed out the cards, everyone held his breath for fear of getting one of these. It was an embarrassed student who opened a card with an ugly ape leering at him and read the verse, "Roses are red, violets are blue, you look like an ape and you live in the zoo."

Parties, too, have changed. Karen and Mark compared their collections of candies and cookies that the room mothers brought as though they were counting out Halloween booty. Four red suckers, a collection of conversation hearts, cinnamon and jelly candies and decorated cookies—and it was all expected! Back in the '40s, we looked forward to homemade decorated heart cookies that someone's mother made, and sometimes the teacher let us have cherry Kool-Aid. It just didn't seem so commercialized then.

After the party, I always sorted my valentines. The best had penny suckers attached. The verse usually read, "I'd be a sucker if I didn't ask you to be mine."

If you really liked a kid, you would send him or her a card that had moving parts on it. You know what I mean—wheels moving on cars, or traffic signals moving up and down, or flowers popping out of flower pots. I used to sort them by kinds. First cards with suckers, then large cards with moving parts, next small cards with moving parts, cards you could fold and stand up, those with a bendable tab at the bottom for a stand, flat ones that wouldn't stand up, and homemade cards (which I turned my nose up at). I displayed my cards all over the house—the mantel, the radio, the buffet and my dresser top.

Mark and Karen sort their cards, too. Mark held up a nice card and commented, "Look Mom, Billy paid good money for this card—it didn't come from a valentine packet like everyone else's. He gave one to every kid in the room."

Mark really thought Billy appreciated him more than his other friends did because he spent more money! I suppose this is one of the facts of life that will carry over with Mark into adulthood. Don't some adults compare the Christmas cards they receive?

Maybe some customs really do change for the better, though. I guess the reason they give out lists of names is to keep some child from feeling hurt.

My dad related how one year, back in the "real old days," his sister didn't get any valentines. He resolved that the following year would be different. He bought a lot of valentines and wrote her name on all of them. He says they never signed their names to the cards in his day. By disguising his handwriting and having some of his friends help put a few valentines in the box, he made sure that Mabel wouldn't be hurt again. To this day she doesn't know how she became the most popular girl in the class that year!

After all, isn't the real purpose of Valentine's Day to show love for our friends and relatives? It's the one time of year we can tell them either humorously or sincerely that we appreciate the little things they do for us without feeling embarrassed.

As yesterday's customs blend with today's new trends, our children, too, are creating memories they will someday relate to their children, for such is the way of life—and that is as it should be! ❖

I couldn't wait another day
To tell you what
I got to say
Don't know how
to tell it
Kinda shy you know
But I'll be happy
VALENTINE
If you'll be my beau

Mary had a little lamb
Whose fleece was white as snow
And like it, my heart follows you
Wherever you may go

May This Dart Pierce Your Heart

By Doris Brecka

There is a lot to be said for progress, but a definite thorn in my side is the effect progress is having on our colorful commemorative days. The hype and commercialism that threaten to spoil Christmas are decried by many.

Halloween fun could very well be eliminated because of the dangers involved with trick-or-treating today. And an especially sore spot is the way Valentine's Day has turned into an occasion when "Them that has, gets," and vice versa.

It wasn't that way in our small rural school. Under the teacher's watchful eyes, we slowly and methodically deposited our 12 to 15 valentines into the gaily decorated pasteboard box on which the "big kids" had labored, savoring the import of the moment.

These valentines were the store-bought variety, though we did create a few originals—usually for parents, grandparents or neighbors—from the teacher's pattern, often a large red heart pierced with a white cupid's arrow, and painstakingly inscribed, "To My Valentine." With February art class also given over to black silhouettes of Washington and Lincoln, hatchets, cherry branches and log cabins, there was hardly time to make valentines for the entire school. And to own a selection of construction paper in one's own home was unheard of.

Back then, a single cent bought a valentine; and for another penny it was sent on its way to a relative.

Back then, a single cent bought a valentine from a wide selection of attractive postcards that could be presented at school or, for another penny, sent on its way to a distant relative. But in general, valentines were of a more delicate and sentimental variety, usually having the shape of a hinged heart, or maybe a rectangle with scalloped edges simulating lace and garnished with violets or rosebuds. The message was tender and romantic. My own favorites were those that opened into honeycomb hearts, but at the cost of somewhere around a quarter, these were only purchased for a well-liked teacher.

In the 20-plus years which elapsed before my own children took valentines to school, the greetings evolved into more cute and cunning types, very often featuring small animals with movable parts, or folding into stand-up valentines with three-dimensional effects.

Youngsters were able to make their personal selections from a dime store counter well supplied with those for a penny each, two for a nickel, or a nickel or a dime apiece. (Was anyone really worth that much?") Envelopes were selected to fit.

I marvel now at the patience of the salesgirl who waited for each child's purchase to be completed, and at that of the mother who often was waiting.

At home, another exciting activity took place as each child lay on his stomach on the parlor carpet, intently selecting the recipient for each valentine, changing his mind with each recollection of what had been received the previous year.

Once the small schools were consolidated into larger ones, there came the problem of exchanging valentines in rooms with 25 or 30 children. The inevitable result was that valentines were given not to everyone, but only to the most popular children. Some of the teachers, no doubt distressed at the heart-rending unfairness, regretfully opted to do away with the custom entirely.

Whenever I think about the "good" in the Good Old Days, I think very often of Valentine's Day. How lucky those of us are who have memories of a day when our school desks held a dozen loving messages, each imploring us, "Be My Valentine."❖

Arbor Day

By Edna P. Bates

The little, one-room, red brick "country school" on the top of the Niagara Escarpment was my school. There was only one teacher for all eight grades, and she taught there for 10 years. Besides the regular classes, she also taught sewing and manual training. In winter, she had us cook hot lunches. She was also a strict disciplinarian, and didn't believe in us wasting a minute.

There was no resident caretaker for the school. A man came and made the fire on winter mornings, and after he started the big, black, potbellied stove, he swept the floor. Just before school started in September, one of the three trustees (who served without pay) came with his team and hay mower and mowed the two months' growth of grass around the school yard. That was the extent of the caretaking. The rest was done by the teacher and pupils. One of us carried a pail of water in each morning from the pump in the school yard. We had graduated from the communal dipper. Our teacher was very germ-conscious, so she had each of us bring our own cup from home.

Our school had a front porch. In winter, we could sweep the snow off our shoes there, and it kept the wind from blowing directly into the schoolroom when we went in the door. Two little outhouses behind the school, one on each side of the yard, provided our "sanitary facilities." The back porch (which years later contained more modern "facilities") was used only for storage, and as a private place to administer justice! Unlike many teachers of the day, ours never punished anyone in front of other pupils. If someone's behavior was not acceptable, she took him or her (no sex discrimination!) onto the back porch. The ominous silence outside was matched by the quiet in the classroom—not a whisper was heard from one of the 35 or 40 pupils! Then we could hear the *thwack*! of the strap. Minutes later, a very subdued pupil would come back and sit down quietly. No one laughed when she strapped!

Everything she did was done thoroughly, but obviously, she did not relish the punishment any more than the "victim" did. Nor did any parents object to the small amount of corporal punishment she meted out. She seldom needed to use it anyway. Most of us just did what she expected of us! She did use sarcasm as a weapon on occasion, though.

One day, after tasting the applesauce that was the "hot lunch" that

Another Arbor Day we discovered two boys who had gone ahead of us and were having an illicit "skinny-dip."

day, my older sister commented, "This applesauce is as sour as pig swill!"

Our teacher remarked dryly, "Sadie, I didn't know you were in the habit of eating pig swill."

We didn't get any "professional development days" off from school back then. We were expected to be in school every day, and do our work. There was just one day that was different: Arbor Day. We still had work to do, but not the same kind. We cleaned the school, inside and out. We raked all the school yard.

When everything was finished to our teacher's satisfaction, then—and only then—came the "fun" part of the day: We all hiked down the side of the escarpment. Two of the older pupils took along a shovel and dug up a small maple tree from the woods. Every year we added another tree to those already in the school yard. While the older students worked, the rest of us just had a good time.

Though my sisters and I often went down the escarpment at home on Sundays, this trip was quite different. It was during "school hours"! We hunted for wildflowers. We ate the little tubers under the "spring beauties," nibbled wild leeks, chewed the bark from the slippery elm trees, ate wintergreen leaves (if we were lucky enough to find any), and anything else that looked palatable! No one was ever poisoned; either we were good judges of our native plants, or we had very hardy stomachs!

The teacher couldn't keep all 35 or 40 of her flock in sight. The tiny ones stayed with her and the rest scattered. Nowadays a trip like that would not be permitted without more supervision, but "way back then," parent volunteers hadn't been heard of—thank goodness!

One Arbor Day, as we went past a neighbor's pond on our way to the woods, we found a raft that his sons had built. Two of the older boys "borrowed" it and took us out, one at a time, for rides. One girl was afraid to go alone and she wanted me to go with her. Once out in the middle of the pond, she panicked, screamed, grabbed me and nearly upset us all. How deep the pond was then, I don't know.

Another Arbor Day, as we came back by the same pond, we discovered two boys who had gone ahead of us and were having an illicit "skinny-dip." This was long before the days of nudity in the movies, so we were very shocked. Having no brothers, I was also quite enlightened! If the teacher had happened by just then, the boys would have been in deeper waters than those of the pond!

By 4 p.m. on Arbor Day, we had all made our way up the steep slopes of the escarpment, through the woods and meadows, back to the school—to the daily world of pencils, books and discipline, to another year of doing what was expected of us, with no arguments. But always ahead, beckoning like a mirage, was the delicious freedom of next year's Arbor Day. ❖

The Golden Egg

By Donna McGuire Tanner

In the early 1950s, my first years of learning were spent at the Pax Elementary School in Pax, W. Va., a once-booming, coal-mining town. Some of our teachers chose to teach us the ways of life from yesterday by showing and doing. One teacher taught us to grow "Depression flowers" on lumps of coal by adding salt and bluing. The same year we learned how to make beanbags, and were allowed to toss them in the classroom after we had finished sewing the beans in the cloth.

One year our Mother's Day project was to carve something out of a cake of soap. I was going to make the easiest object possible, a cross. But with a quick slip of the knife, I found one side of the soap gone. My mother, Rachel, loved the yellow soap canary that I made for her.

The most difficult object we were expected to make was a braided rug, made from strips of old clothes we had brought from home. Several of us were in a group working on one rug. We used our time at recesses and lunchtime to complete it.

Truthfully, I now know it was something no one would want to put in their home. It had a big bulge in the center, but we were proud of it. My group gave it to me to take home. Mom didn't wipe away my smile when I gave it to her. She put it on the living-room floor for all to see.

In the fifth grade, I needed a nature project. I was at a loss as to what to do. Most of my classmates were gathering leaves or wildflowers. My grandmother, Bertha Workman, took me to her beloved flower garden. She showed me how to cut a snip of one of her flowers. Then she instructed me to take it to school and put it in a glass of water. I really didn't know what was going to happen. Soon, to my amazement, and to the delight of my teacher, it grew roots. I got an A for the simple show of how nature worked.

Once we were told to bring a large potato to school. We thought we were going to cook something. Instead, we cut the potatoes in halves. Then we carved designs of flowers or animals. We dipped the potatoes in paint and pressed them onto paper, creating a collage of individual originality.

Of all the handicrafts that we made in my elementary school years, I remember the golden Easter eggs best of all.

At Christmastime, we usually made our classroom decorations from red and green construction paper. It was a challenge to see how long we could make the paper chain.

A wise teacher insisted we make our own valentines and give everyone in the class one. She probably realized most of us came from large families where money was best not wasted on valentines.

Of all the handicrafts that we made in my elementary school years, I remember the golden Easter eggs best of all.

A few days before Easter we received the unusual homework assignment, and the instructions on how to do it. That evening Mom helped me wrap an egg in golden onion peels. Then we bound it tightly in a clean cloth. Gently we tied strings around the cloth to bind the egg and hold it securely together. Next we put the egg in water and boiled it. Since it was wrapped in a cloth, we allowed 45 minutes to an hour of gentle boiling.

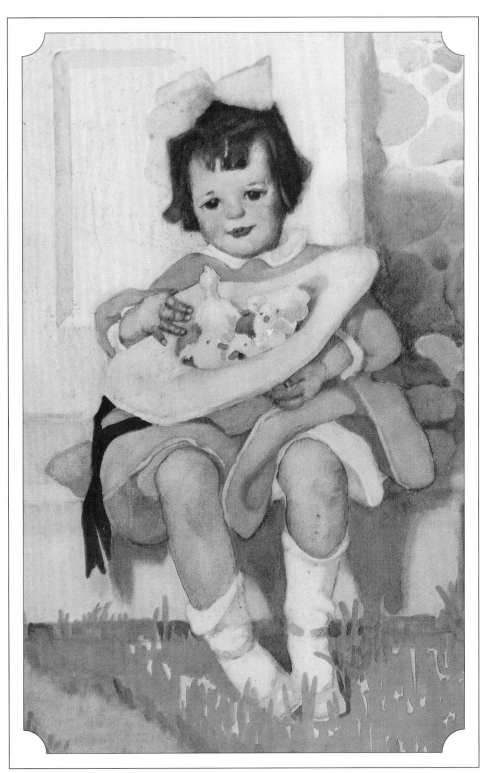

After the egg cooled, we removed the layers of wet cloth and onion peels. I was awed by the golden object I held in my hand.

At school the following day, we made a display of our golden eggs. No two were alike. Some had green blended in the gold from the green on the onion peel. Our teacher told us that this was the way children colored eggs for Easter before they had dye.

Golden Easter eggs became a tradition in our family. And I was glad that my teachers had passed on their own Good Old Days.❖

Decoration Day, 1910

By Virginia Moy

The commemoration exercises for Decoration Day, 1910, on May 26 and 27 at Berkeley, Calif., where I attended grammar school, were memorable and inspirational.

Although Decoration Day—our present Memorial Day—was actually May 28, we had special school programs on Thursday morning, the 26th, and Friday morning, the 27th. Each day, we were fortunate to have important guests: officers who had served in the Civil War of 1861–1865 and in the Spanish-American War of 1898.

Since we had no auditorium, the heavy folding doors were pushed open between classrooms. To accommodate all of the pupils, two children sat at each desk. As we entered the room Thursday morning, we noticed our four guests sitting in the front of the room—two officers of the Union army and two officers of the Confederate army. We were able to identify which was which, as we had learned the song *The Men in Blue and Gray.* The Unionists, in their full dress uniforms, related stories about Abraham Lincoln, General Grant and some important battles in which they had fought, especially the Battle of Gettysburg. (The older students were proud then that they had learned the *Gettysburg Address.*) The Confederate officers, also wearing their dress uniforms, spoke of General Lee, the march through Georgia, and some of the hardships they had endured. These feeble men, close to 80 years of age, supported themselves by leaning against the podium as they spoke to us. We were old enough to be attentive, but we did not hear what they tried to tell us, for their voices were weak and whispery. However, we never did forget those uniformed men in blue and gray who gave so generously of themselves.

So dramatic was our first speaker and so excited were we that we sat on the edges of our seats.

For our part of the program, we sang appropriate songs: *Tenting on the Old Camp Ground, Battle Hymn of the Republic,* and *My Country 'Tis of Thee* (that was the only name I knew for the song, although it was our national anthem at that time).

For the next two years, the Civil War officers returned to visit us on Decoration Day, not to participate in our program, but simply as very tired, old soldiers whose fading memories were rekindled by the familiar songs we sang for them.

On Friday morning, our guest speakers were two of Theodore Roosevelt's Rough Riders of 1898. How eagerly we listened as our first

<table>
LINCOLN CENTENNIAL
SOUVENIR
1809   1909

ABRAHAM LINCOLN
THE MARTYRED PRESIDENT.

From the humblest origin, by zeal and personal worth,
he reached the highest pinnacle of fame.
His name will ever shine pre-eminently in
history as the Champion of Liberty.

COPYRIGHT 1908 BY E.
</table>

Our second speaker of the morning told us stories about the organizer of the Rough Riders—"Teddy" Roosevelt, as he was affectionately known. We were especially interested in Teddy's love of bears, and in the fact that he often had his picture taken with a bear cub. At that time, a new toy, a cuddly bear, was put on the Christmas market.

"Guess what the bear's name was?" asked our guest. "He was called, 'Teddy Bear.' " How surprised we were, for some of us did own a teddy bear.

Friday afternoon was the highlight of our program. After lunch, most students returned to school bearing brightly-colored wreaths which they had made from their own garden flowers which bloomed profusely. This project had been assigned earlier in the week. We assembled in the school yard and then our teachers led us in double file out onto the Berkeley Wharf. There we saw the Marine band, our six visitors from the previous days, the mayor, our school principal and a local minister. The flag was flying at half-mast. When we were quietly assembled, the Marine band played *Not Costly Domes Nor Marble Towers Shall Mark the Place Where Heroes Sleep*, *Battle Hymn of the Republic* and other songs we had learned in school. Then the minister led us in prayer.

speaker narrated the glorious victory at San Juan Hill, in Cuba. The corps of volunteers who performed this stupendous feat was the most famous regiment of the Spanish-American War.

So dramatic was our first speaker and so excited were we that we sat on the edges of our seats, gripped the arms of our chairs, and literally ran with him up San Juan Hill to help win that notorious victory. (The Rough Riders were long remembered after the war of '98 since senior men at the University of California at Berkeley wore authentic Rough Rider hats as their class distinction.) The great victory at San Juan Hill was an important factor when Roosevelt was campaigning for the presidency. In fact, San Juan was instrumental in his becoming our 26th president.

So awed were we students by the solemnity of this occasion that we stood quietly waiting to share our contribution to the program. While the band played *Nearer My God to Thee*, we moved to the wharf's railings and tossed our wreaths into San Francisco Bay. The water was at high tide, and we watched our floral offerings ride the crest of the waves out to the watery graves of our unknown but not unsung heroes who were "rocked in the cradle of the deep, where they lay down in peace to sleep." For half an hour we watched our wreaths drift away. Then school was dismissed.

The 1910 Decoration Day commemorative exercises occurred a long time ago, but they remain among my most memorable and inspirational treasures.❖

One Humiliated Spirit!

By Robert J. Longfellow

Each year our rural Kansas school prepared an elaborate extravaganza to celebrate May Day. However, looking back and recalling the teacher, Miss McKirkle, I honestly believe she set a trap to get even with the bunch of ornery kids she had taught.

The theme was celebrating the arrival of spring in all its beauty. A group of girls were selected to do the maypole. They were directed to make their dresses in the school colors of green and yellow.

The boys had been herded into a singing group. White shirts and blue pants were a must. The words to two long songs had to be memorized, the second to be sung only in the event they had a curtain call.

Being small for my age, I thought I had escaped being involved in the production. Anyway, I was shy and timid. Just the thought of standing in front of mothers and fathers weakened my knees.

But I was caught when Miss McKirkle informed me I was to be the "Spirit of Spring." I would open the production. From a large box she dug out short green pants and a frizzly-looking green pullover garment with dozens of little bells sewn on the collar and sleeves. To top it off, she produced a green pointed hat that had a big tulip secured to the point.

I cringed at the thought of wearing this crazy outfit and let it be known I wasn't about to do so. Later, Miss McKirkle had a talk with my dad. As Dad put it, I was to be the Spirit of Spring—or else!

My part required me to lightly leap out from the wings, saying, "I am the Spirit of Spring. Ah, Spring, you make us so happy." I was to wave my flower-covered wand and, to the tune of *Old McDonald*, sing: "The birds are singing merrily and the little buds are bursting on the trees." Then I was to skip off the stage and the curtain would be pulled open, starting the first act.

The opening night arrived. Mothers and fathers filled the little area and soon quieted down, anticipating the evening's entertainment. The cast were in their places, and I felt sick standing there in my Spring outfit. Before I could escape through the open window, Miss McKirkle gently but firmly pushed me out onto the stage. As if a switch had been turned on, I went into my act.

I leaped about, waving the wand, and shouted, "I'm the Spirit of Spring! Ah, Spring, you make us very happy!" After a few more awkward leaps, I continued, "The birds are busting on the trees and the little buds are singing merrily!"

This brought laughter from the audience. I knew I had messed up. I kept thinking bigger leaps would get me off the stage quicker. My last leap was a bit higher than the others, which caused those darned Spring pants to fall to my ankles! With the sound of little bells tinkling, I slid off the stage on my belly.

When the audience learned I hadn't been injured, they applauded and cheered with laughter. Miss McKirkle put her arm around me. "Bobbie, all great actors have had their bad moments, but they get over it. You were so good, I believe we'll have a comedy show next year!"❖

May Day! May Day!

By Betty Hatcher

In the '30s and '40s, May Day didn't remind us of desperate planes and ships shouting an alert. It wasn't military parades in Red Square or honoring the judicial system in America.

Each May Day in my teens, I was up by dawn to wash my face in the dew, a guarantee of beauty. Of course, I really didn't believe that fable. On the other hand, I wasn't going to miss the chance, just in case it could work.

When the calendar said the first day of May had arrived, it was the culmination of weeks of work and scores of prayers for good weather by faculty, students and associated parents of our junior high school.

During the bleak days of January through March, the hallways were blasted by *Dance of the Flowers* issuing from the band room, competing with the chorus who harmonized to *Melody in F* with: "Welcome, sweet springtime, We greet thee with song. … " By the time the day arrived, even the tone-deaf had learned all the words and hummed along.

The May Queen was always the beauty whose mother kept her hair in golden ringlets. My straight-as-a-board hair eliminated me; it couldn't hold a curl for 15 minutes. My hope was to be one of the "flowers" who crouched in ranks, faces framed by crepe-paper "petals"— yellow jonquils, purple pansies, pink sweet peas and red tulips. The rest of the year we could tell who had been chosen because their white gym shoes were dyed green. Oh, how I wished for green tennis shoes!

My last year in junior high school, I was down to one unchewed fingernail when Miss Blake got around to me.

> *The May Queen was always the beauty whose mother kept her hair in golden ringlets.*

"Betty, what are we going to do with you? You're still growing. Well, it's the maypole for you once more." Her hand on my shoulder was kind, but I was doomed to white gym shoes.

Every year the janitor constructed two 10-foot poles and nailed long strips of pastel cloth to the tops. In three years, my maypole had never wound the ribbons down the pole. Once the apparatus even fell over, to the delight of the audience, but to our chagrin—and the janitor's.

There were no opportunities to practice with the actual pole. Our instructions came on the gym floor as we wove in and out around a circle. It was a strain on us and Miss Blake. The boys were not interested in "this sissy stuff." The girls so chosen were odd shapes and sizes who did not fit the flower ranks and couldn't sing. The only requirement was a white shirt for the boys and a white dress for the girls. Even in the depths of the Depression, we all could meet those standards.

My last May Day celebration dawned clear and bright. Ranks of parents on folding chairs edged the school lawn and the excitement was noisy. The school band had blown its way through the march that led the Queen of May on the arm of her king to gilded thrones on the school steps. (Even I could have been graceful hanging onto that jock.)

The chorus wriggled on bleacher tiers center stage and began their song to springtime as the West Wind trailed her scarves between rows of green tennis shoes. It really was effective as the flower faces lifted and stretched upward, reaching for the sky.

Finally it was time for the grand finale, the

maypoles. As we took our places, I felt the familiar clutch in my stomach. When the band began with a clash of brass, I realized they had switched music on us. Now it was *Country Dances*—and too fast. I eyed Miss Blake, who looked pale as she gave the signal.

Jimmy, the roly-poly redhead in front of me, was waving at his parents behind me. I gave him a punch, which did not turn him in the right direction but brought him an angry step toward me. The boy behind me was treading on my heels, hissing, "Go on!"

Jimmy, never swift to change ideas, finally reversed, but by then the fat girl in front of him was five feet away. He ran to catch up, then forgot whether to go inside or out. I skipped forward and bodily shoved him inside. The snickers from parents were louder than the band.

The boy behind passed on my left and it was my turn to go inside—but there was no one there! It was the old nightmare again I'd fought three years running. The ribbon of pink fabric was wet in my hand and I felt drops oozing down my armpit.

Forget them all, I told myself and slipped into the rhythm of the gym practices. In and out, in and out I went, surprised to find I was steady on my feet. Jimmy finally had gotten the hang of it and our circle grew smaller as the pastels wound down the pole. Soon the ribbons were so short we were as crouched as the flowers had been center stage. We dropped the strands and stood.

I glanced at the second maypole. It teetered precariously. The dancers were bunched together on one side, fighting their way through the congestion. Their colored streamers were braiding into one long ponytail which did not involve the pole. The audience convulsed and the dancers giggled. Band members began to chuckle. When they no longer could pucker for a note, one by one the instruments faded away. With the last duet of clarinet and tuba, the band director dropped his arms and joined the hilarity. We certainly had greeted "sweet springtime with laughter and song."

I looked up at our neatly braided maypole and the pastel colors smiled at me. At last I had had a part in something that turned out right. When parents began to seek their own, in the confusion before Mom and Dad met me, I felt a hand on my shoulder.

"Betty, you led them beautifully," Miss Blake said. "That's the first time in four years a maypole succeeded. Thank you."

That was the year I kept my gym shoes white with pride. I was a successful maypole dancer. I'd finally grown in to my feet. Since that day I've no longer felt I was made up of spare parts.

I miss those May Day celebrations. Something fine and gentle has disappeared from our culture. ❖

Graduation, 1928

By Raymond E. Schiesser

January, 1928 marked my graduation from Public School 88 at the corner of Catalpa Ave. and Silver St., Ridgewood, Brooklyn, N.Y. How well I remember those faces of yesteryears, the Tim hats, the knickers and long stockings. Henry Holzbach was one of our class's gifted artists. Howard Tobin, who became a Marine and a World War II hero in the South Pacific, was another. I ran about a sad fifth in that category.

Virginia Rohlich, Katherine Graybusch and Helen Nestler were among the smartest girls. Anna Kunert was a whiz who skipped four classes. Eva Maczkowski, Eleanor Kleiner, Marie Monz, Kathleen Pflug, Catherine Fisher and the Kennedy sisters, Anna and Dorothy, were the class beauties.

Al Rosesco, who would be on the United States Olympic field hockey team in 1936, set the class mark for never being absent or late, with 13 consecutive perfect terms. Howard Tobin and I were second with 10 terms. Measles and whooping cough marred my early years. Charles Shaw, who was often troubled with boils, was the strongest boy and our best broad-jumper. Only principal Jacob Rohrback could best his record in the latter.

I will always remember the teachers who almost broke my left arm with rulers and pointers so I would learn to write right-handed.

Ed Werner, who played football later with the Ridgewood Red Wings, was the quickest with a quip. John Andress, our class vice president and a good basketball player, served unharmed through all the major Pacific naval battles of World War II, only to die a few years after his discharge. James McCoy, who always came to school with buns (a forerunner of the coffee break), was our "Dapper Dan" in the knickers of those days. Paul Schmitchen and Al Rosesco were our Boy Scout enthusiasts. Al eventually became the patrol leader of the Lion Patrol of Troop 7.

Fred Stroebel, Walter Mergardt, Fred Diers and I were the class shrimps. All of us, save Walter, received our share of Irish toothaches. Our Ed Behrman's brother, Hank, pitched for the Brooklyn Dodgers baseball team in 1946 and 1947. The two Henrys, Schardt and Wenz, were the Phil Silvers of their day with hilarious jokes and snappy patter, while Paul Velte was the Gary Cooper of that day. One must never forget Lois Hammersley, our star swimmer. We sometimes envisioned her as another Gertrude Ederle.

At a penny candy store across the street from the school, Eric Hauptman and William Walsh spent their pennies buying new tricks. I preferred to spend my penny for a pretzel from the basket of the old German gentleman who stood on the corner of Silver St. in all kinds of weather. His wares were always covered with a cloth towel. Funny, even though I am 61 today, I still enjoy a pretzel from a street vendor, even if the price has gone up.

My classmates and I were movie fans and loved adventure stories. Our most adventurous member was David Lotner, who was born between Russia and Poland in 1911. Ruffians later broke into his house, took whatever they wanted and set the house afire. David's family loaded a wagon with clothes, bread and wine, and fled for their lives. They lived in a forest for two years until they were able to make their way to the village of his grandfather from which they later emigrated to America. David later became a successful grocer.

Keller, Harry Farbach, Richard Schmid, Clara Koehler, Julia Essex, Adelle Schall and Les Grim, the grocer's son, were also in our graduation class of 1928. I can still see James McCoy, William Wetzel and Fred Diers marching across the stage, portraying *The Spirit of '76.* Seemed strange to see immaculate James looking so dirty.

Charles Shaw was our class president as well as victor over tough Caspar Baum in a savage school-yard scrap. Charlie was very popular, except with Miss Rupp, our music teacher. Miss Rupp always made us sing *Charlie Is My Darling*. Charlie never cottoned to that song and brought tears to Miss Rupp's eyes with his very loud rendition.

After Charles made his speech on that January day, the salutatory was given by Katherine Graybusch. I was a pilgrim in the cantata, part three, *The Coming of the Pilgrims*. Virginia Rohlich, always an excellent speaker, made the Thanksgiving speech. Eli Melanofsky, who would someday be a famous lawyer, eloquently recited Patrick Henry's famous address. And last but never least, was Valentine Neumann's rendition of *The Ride of Paul Revere*. American history was our forté in those days, and I still think American history is the greatest.

> *How were we to know then that 1929 and the Depression would be a barrier to our progress?*

The graduation address was given by my pastor, Carl Hirzel of Covenant Lutheran Church. He regaled us with tales of his youthful baseball-playing days and the terrible tragedy when the one and only baseball was lost in the tall grass. He compared that escapade to life, telling us that our future lay ahead of us.

"Part the tall grass," he said. "See the vastness of the horizon beyond beckoning to you. Who knows? Perhaps one of you, like I, will feel the call to the ministry, but whatever path you choose, God's blessing goes with you for success in the future." Having finished, he bowed his head and said a short prayer.

How strange it seemed to stand on the stage and see some of my teachers sitting amidst the parents in the audience. I saw Dennis Regan, the shop teacher who always kept oranges in his desk drawer. A few rows beyond him sat Mrs. Lillian Ledwide; I always did well in her composition class. She had instructed Anna Goyanovick and me to write the class farewell poem. This is the last stanza:

"So long to 88 awhile,
  Good luck, Old Red and Black,
  No matter where or when we go,

Someday we will come back."

I caught sight of Miss Rowland, who on her first sight of me expressed the wish that I would be as good a student as my brother, Nicholas—I was. Then there was the science teacher, Mrs. Badetti, who hoped I would be a better student than my brother, Nicholas—I wasn't. Of course, there was Miss Margaret Cahill, who once, in the fourth grade, lifted me out of my seat by my chin. I spotted Paul Noller and Mr. Zenner, the athletic teachers who were always aces.

I will always remember the teachers who almost broke my left arm with rulers and pointers so I would learn to write right-handed. It was hard to believe I was leaving "88." How I would miss looking into all those wonderful stores on the way to and from school. Let's see; there was Messner's Candy Store, Meyer's Ice Cream Parlor, Merkel's Moving, Ferdinand Zoeller's barbershop and Ed Sullivan's hardware store. Who could forget the lobsters wriggling in the window of Chiote's Restaurant, the French fries in the deep fat of Elsasser's fish store and the smell of Rustman's rye bread coming from the bakery on Silver Street?

And on Cornelia Street, I always heard music coming from the Jasmagy Music Studio where Ruth and Clarence Jasmagy instructed pupils. Oh, yes, and the wonderful world of the John Hancock Insurance office next to the Fresh Pond elevated, where history pamphlets could be procured. I regret that I never saved one of them.

How were we to know then that 1929 and the Depression would be a barrier to our progress? And if we had known, would we have cared? It was a happy time then and we were proud to receive our diplomas. We signed each other's autograph books and entered Moglich's Ice Cream Parlor for our final get-together.

Yes, that's how it was in January of 1928, and to you, John Andress and Howard Tobin, up there in the sky of blue above us, rest assured we think of you. ❖

Schoolrooms & School Yards

Chapter Four

———⟫◇⟪———

*L*ike millions of others across this great North American continent, my life was molded and shaped by my experiences in the schoolroom and school yard of my youth.

Today's gangs are yesterday's bullies, and I learned how to handle a bully on the playground. James was our school bully and he chose me to humiliate day after day until one fateful recess after Christmas. That was when he broke a toy car Santa had brought me. Bully James found a hellion. He went screaming for the teacher and I learned to never back down from a bully.

Affairs of the heart are the same, generation to generation. Ours were just a lot more innocent then. I thought I had won Mary Lynn's affections when I only chased her in a game of freeze tag. Then came Valentine's Day. Mary Lynn didn't get me the big valentine I had seen at the general store. Heck, she didn't even draw me an arrow-pieced heart on a stupid piece of paper. That was how I learned to deal with rejection in the third grade.

Probably the most important life lesson I learned from my experiences in that country school, however, was the one about gambling. I had become a regular high roller by the time I was in fourth grade. First, it was pitching pennies, then flipping nickels. But one day I made the mistake of playing marbles for "keepsies" with Sally.

I knew Sally was a good marble player, but she was a girl and no girl could beat me! She held an impressive bag of agates, but her shooter was what interested me. It was the best shooter I had seen anywhere. We made a bet: Whoever captured the most marbles from the ring drawn in the school yard dirt would win the other's shooter. It was a daring gamble for me; I had had my shooter for over a year and it had never failed in the ring of competition.

The game began innocently enough. Sally and I exchanged several good runs, then I edged slightly into the lead about midway through the match. That's when the roof caved in. Sally punched out a good run of eight marbles or so and claimed a pretty good lead in marbles. I only got back three or four on my next round, while Sally pulled farther ahead with another good run. I did the math— I needed almost all of the last dozen marbles to keep from losing my shooter.

It was probably sweat pouring off my forehead onto my shooting hand that caused the shooter to slip after just the third shot in my next round. Sally removed all suspense by smashing four agates from the ring for the insurmountable lead. With the pressure off, I finished off what was left of the marbles and then begrudgingly handed Sally my shooter. Then and there I swore off gambling.

Those experiences of a lifetime are still with me. James taught me that most bullies are just cowards deep down. Mary Lynn—that hussy—helped me recognize true love when it came along in the form of my dear wife, Janice, a few years later. And, because of Sally, I have never had the temptation of playing the slots at Vegas or Reno. I learned from her to keep my money on the sure bets of life: God, family, good friends—love that lasts forever. Yes, I learned a lot in those schoolrooms and on those school yards back in a time called the Good Old Days.
—Ken Tate

Crime & Punishment

By Guinevere Koppler

Seventy years ago, or perhaps not so long ago as that, a boy caught throwing a paper wad, or loitering along the way and arriving late for school, might end up getting a good paddling. If it were a country school, the paddling might take place in front of the entire school. This was no guarantee that the culprit would never do it again, but it did keep some of the spectators on the straight and narrow.

It wasn't the paddling so much as the audience. There is something about being seen pulled across the teacher's lap and having one's backside chastised that is very humiliating. Today, it seems that punishment consists of being sent from the room (which is what the culprit wanted in the first place), or being expelled (which is even better), or getting an F for the day's work. The culprit, instead of being shamed, now often brags about how he "showed the teacher up."

In the school I attended as a child, the youngster caught throwing a paper wad or committing some other misdemeanor was sent to the superintendent's office. Here the offender was told to bend over a chair, and he was given several whacks across the seat of his pants with a paddle (referred to by students as "the board of education"). Some of the more theatrical miscreants yelled quite loudly to give the rest of us a few laughs and show they weren't hurt too badly.

Some of the more theatrical miscreants yelled loudly to give the rest of us a few laughs and show they weren't hurt too badly.

Once there was a great deal of excitement when one boy had a box of matches in his back pocket. After a few whacks, the matches caught on fire and had to be put out amid yells and snickers.

We girls were a giggly group with many secrets to relate. These secrets often came to mind during study periods and we were caught whispering (a deadly sin at that time).

One enterprising young lady teacher made placards which said, "I am a whisperer" on them, which she made us wear around our necks. It was as bad as if it had read "I have the plague." While our girlfriends were more often very sympathetic, boys would follow us around, shaking their fingers at us.

I remember one little girl who sat across from a boy on whom she had quite a crush. She kept trying to get his attention by rather loud whispering. Miss Williams, the teacher, endured it for a while and then finally said, "Margaret, if you want to be with Richard so bad, sit with him."

A tearful Margaret sat in Richard's seat with him while he tried hard to appear nonchalant.

Once, a boy caught whispering was told to write "I will not whisper" 100 times. I sat near him and he showed me the paper on which he was doing his task; he had written "I will not whisper" once at the top of the page, and underneath he had numbered 100 lines and used ditto marks. It was just a joke; he had another paper numbered to 100 on which he intended to write the correct lines, but the teacher caught him and looked at the first page. She was not amused. She told him to write 200 hundred lines.

And, oh, to be caught chewing gum! Punishment ranged from wearing the gum stuck on the end of one's nose or forehead, or even one's ear, to chewing in front of the class for a given period without stopping. (This was very hard on the mouth and jaws.) Worst of all were the lectures and threats directed at the next person who dared to bring gum to class.

Many who never thought of chewing gum in class did other things nearly as bad (at least in the view of our teacher). Chewing one's nails was a terrible thing, but chewing one's pencil was almost as bad as gum. One teacher kept a pacifier in her desk drawer and delighted in sneaking up on a young thinker who was nervously chewing away, grabbing the pencil from his mouth, and putting the pacifier in its place. I remember having it in my own mouth once and wondering fearfully about germs. I was afraid to ask, but I hoped she washed it off after each time she used it.

Once, two boys found spitting on the sidewalk in front of the school were forced into a spitting contest to see which one could spit the farthest and the most. Then they were told to get pails of water and brooms and scrub the sidewalks. Spitting wasn't nearly so much fun after that.

Mispronouncing words or laughing at great writers was punishable by various means, mostly ridicule. In second grade, there was one girl who, when reading *Peter Rabbit,* always

pronounced the farmer's name as "Mr. McJigger." Those of us who laughed were considered as guilty as the reader. And those who got tickled reciting from *Hiawatha* were often told to stand in the corner for failing to appreciate the "Gichee-Gumee's" and other beauties of poetry.

In history class, when we first heard about the great General Bonaparte, the very smartest girl in our class (who for once hadn't been listening, according to the teacher) pronounced his first name "Nap-po-lene," and became the butt of endless jokes. It seems silly now, but the question, "Have you had your nap, Polene?" sent her into spasms of rage. Once, in the third grade, a friend had given me a yellow delicious apple that I put in my desk. It looked so tempting just lying there that every once in a while I took a nice bite out of it. I was chewing away with stealthy pleasure when I was spied by the teacher. For punishment, I was not allowed to eat with the rest of the children at noon. While they ate in happy groups, I had to sit by myself. As a result, I ate as quickly as possible and finished off the apple, which, by then, was a little sour.

Those who couldn't write by Palmer method and hold the pen in a certain way had their fingers rapped by a ruler—painful! Anyone who started to answer a question with "Well … " was cautioned that there was no time to dig a well before answering. I could never see the humor in this as I was one of the offenders.

If we misspelled a word, we were told to look it up in the dictionary. I once asked a teacher, "If I can't spell it, how will I know when I find it?" I was serious, but the teacher thought I was trying to be funny, and she gave me the same look I might have expected after uttering a four-letter word.

The word "ain't" worked its way into our dictionary against the will of many a strong-minded teacher. Anyone caught saying the word was immediately shouted at. "There is no such word!" one irate teacher told a boy, who,

> *Those who couldn't write by Palmer method and hold the pen in a certain way had their fingers rapped by a ruler—painful!*

I believe, said it as often as he dared to tease her.

He was a smart aleck, but a likable one, and so, to our collective delight, he stated, "If there ain't no such word as ain't how come I can say it?"

As we all laughed and cheered him, the poor teacher got so rattled she fairly screamed, "If I say there ain't no such word as ain't, there ain't!" and went down in red-faced defeat, slumped in her chair.

One had to be careful in writing themes. New ideas were not always popular. We were once told to write a theme on "How I Make Spending Money." Most of us offered very dull contributions about babysitting, going on errands, mowing yards, and helping out at home. One boy, ahead of his time, wrote a glowing account of how he loaned his allowance money to his mother and his older brother and charged them interest. We were all sitting up straight in our seats wondering why we hadn't thought of the same idea.

After he had finished reading his paper and was smirking at his own ingenuity, the teacher lit into him in all her fury. It was, she agreed, all right to treat his brother in such a way because his brother should not have been borrowing in the first place, but to charge his mother interest! Didn't she wash his clothes, mend his socks, cook his meals, and take care of him when he was ill? How could he have the nerve to do such a thing? The money-minded boy sank down in his seat, chagrined, while the rest of us decided he hadn't had such a bright idea after all.

We wore dunce caps, stood in corners, and we stood with our nose in a ring drawn on the blackboard. Each teacher seemed to have her own particular method. Some worked; some didn't. I have heard of old-time cruelty, but in the '20s and '30s, when I was in school, I never saw anything that was meant to be cruel. We were told "Spare the rod and spoil the child," and our teachers and parents lived by it. It has left us with many memories, more humorous than terrible.❖

Boy, Did I Get Spanked!

By Joseph Lane

remember my good old school days. I had a habit of pulling the girls' long hair. I was marched by my ear up to the front of the classroom, and there I was placed across the teacher's knee and soundly spanked with a big, thick paddle.

To make it more embarrassing, she took my little knee pants down before the whole class and spanked my bare little backside with the paddle. I was only 9 years old then. The kids got a big kick out of watching me get spanked—and I mean *spanked*—with that paddle. Many times, I had gone over her knee before the class but, then again, so were others.

The teacher had an old saying, "Spare the rod and spoil the child." She did her best in those days to see I wasn't spoiled. She spared not the rod on my little bare backside until I couldn't sit down. I got spanked for swearing, smoking, skipping school and sassing the teacher back. Oh, I could name dozens of other things for which I was spanked in those days.

I will never forget the time I put some glue on a girl's seat. When she sat down she screamed right out. The teacher came down to see what was wrong. "Oh, that is a terrible thing to do," she said.

The girl said, "I know the brat who did this."

"Point him out to me, Joan," the teacher said.

"Over there—that boy, Joe," Joan said.

So the teacher came over and grabbed me by the ear. "Come up front with me, little boy."

She took the paddle out of the desk drawer and put me across her knee. Boy, did I get spanked that day! Out of all the spankings I got, that was the worst and hardest.

Back then I resented those whippings, but I came to realize that they certainly impressed upon me the difference between right and wrong. Perhaps if there were a little less sparing of the rod today, we wouldn't have so many spoiled children.❖

John
Slobodnik

The Autograph Book

By Virginia Hearn Machir

Back in 1931, when I was a high-school student in Missouri, Hoover was president, Mary Pickford was playing on the screen, there were no free school buses, and every student owned an autograph book in which classmates wrote a verse or a bit of nonsense.

I had to walk a mile down a country lane, where I waited for the old Model-A Ford sedan to pick me up and take me to school in the next town 12 miles away. The driver picked up four more students and we rode merrily along the bumpy gravel road, singing *I'm in Love With You, Honey* or *Dancing Cheek to Cheek* or some other hit of the day.

The three boys always rode in the front seat and the three girls in the back, and they teased us constantly. Sometimes after school, just as we girls almost reached the old Model-A, the three boys would already be in the front seat and would drive away, yelling, "Goodbye! Have a nice walk home!" Sometimes it was 20 or 30 minutes before they returned, and we thought for sure they had left us to walk home. Some days we had a flat tire and had to stop and patch the tube; then we were late for school. Other times, Big Sandy Creek reached flood stage and we were unable to get across, as there was no bridge. The road just went down into the creek bed and out on the other bank. Then we turned and went home and missed school, or we waited a few hours for the floodwaters to subside, and arrived late at school.

> *Every student owned an autograph book in which classmates wrote a verse or a bit of nonsense.*

There was no heater in the old Model-A. We girls put a quilt over our laps in the winter to keep warm. But we never seemed to mind the hardships of riding to and from school, and we enjoyed attending classes in the little country high school.

Following are some verses and bits of fiddle-faddle copied from my old 1931 autograph book. Names have been changed to protect the privacy of my classmates.

Dear Virginia,
I wish you luck, I wish you joy,
I wish you first a baby boy,
And when his hair begins to curl,
I wish you then a baby girl.
Love, Ann

Dear Virginia,
Dorene is my name,
Winfield is my station,
I'm yours 'till death,
Although we are no relation.
A true friend, Dorene

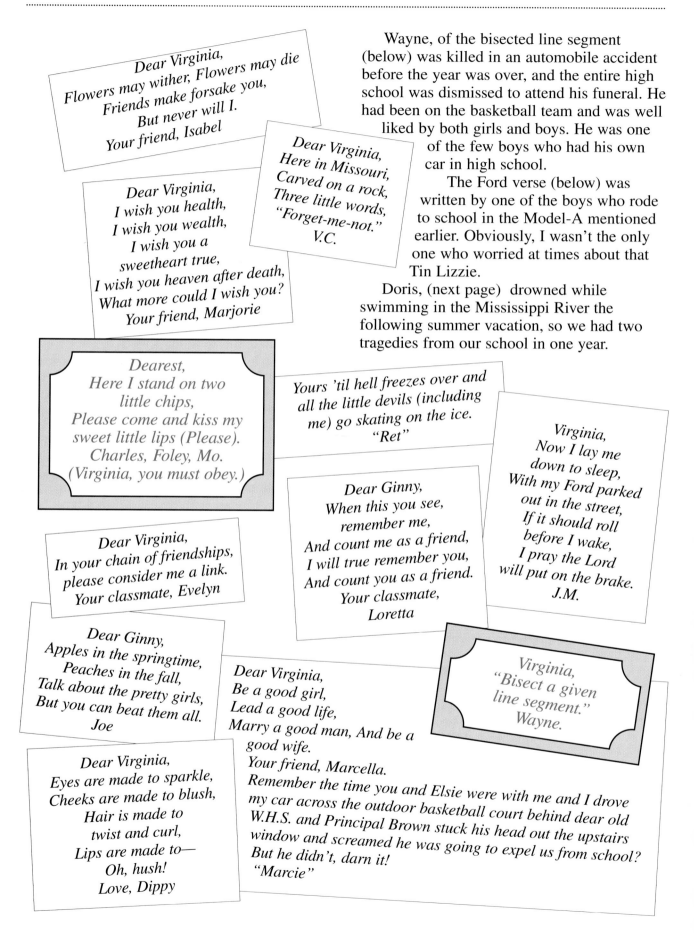

Dear Virginia,
Flowers may wither, Flowers may die
Friends make forsake you,
But never will I.
Your friend, Isabel

Dear Virginia,
I wish you health,
I wish you wealth,
I wish you a
sweetheart true,
I wish you heaven after death,
What more could I wish you?
Your friend, Marjorie

Dear Virginia
Here in Missouri,
Carved on a rock,
Three little words,
"Forget-me-not."
V.C.

Dearest,
Here I stand on two
little chips,
Please come and kiss my
sweet little lips (Please).
Charles, Foley, Mo.
(Virginia, you must obey.)

Yours 'til hell freezes over and
all the little devils (including
me) go skating on the ice.
"Ret"

Dear Virginia,
In your chain of friendships,
please consider me a link.
Your classmate, Evelyn

Dear Ginny,
When this you see,
remember me,
And count me as a friend,
I will true remember you,
And count you as a friend.
Your classmate,
Loretta

Virginia,
Now I lay me
down to sleep,
With my Ford parked
out in the street,
If it should roll
before I wake,
I pray the Lord
will put on the brake.
J.M.

Dear Ginny,
Apples in the springtime,
Peaches in the fall,
Talk about the pretty girls,
But you can beat them all.
Joe

Dear Virginia,
Be a good girl,
Lead a good life,
Marry a good man, And be a
good wife.
Your friend, Marcella.
Remember the time you and Elsie were with me and I drove
my car across the outdoor basketball court behind dear old
W.H.S. and Principal Brown stuck his head out the upstairs
window and screamed he was going to expel us from school?
But he didn't, darn it!
"Marcie"

Virginia,
"Bisect a given
line segment."
Wayne.

Dear Virginia,
Eyes are made to sparkle,
Cheeks are made to blush,
Hair is made to
twist and curl,
Lips are made to—
Oh, hush!
Love, Dippy

Wayne, of the bisected line segment (below) was killed in an automobile accident before the year was over, and the entire high school was dismissed to attend his funeral. He had been on the basketball team and was well liked by both girls and boys. He was one of the few boys who had his own car in high school.

The Ford verse (below) was written by one of the boys who rode to school in the Model-A mentioned earlier. Obviously, I wasn't the only one who worried at times about that Tin Lizzie.

Doris, (next page) drowned while swimming in the Mississippi River the following summer vacation, so we had two tragedies from our school in one year.

I remember Mary. She had a terrific crush on Frank, who sat behind me in study hall. She wrote Frank notes and gave them to me to hand to him during study hall. He answered and gave them to me to hand back to her.

I never read their notes, but Frank thought I did. One day he handed me a note, which I thought was for Mary, and I slipped it to her without reading it. Frank had written the note to me, asking for a date, he later told me. Needless to say, Mary never spoke to me again.

She skipped school for three days and mailed Frank a letter, threatening suicide. Three weeks later, her broken heart had healed and she was wearing the class ring of one of the star basketball players. After that episode, I never played mail carrier for any of my classmates again.

In 1973, my husband and I happened to be driving through Winfield and I asked him to drive up the hill so I could have a look at my old high school. To my surprise, where the old, two-story brick building had stood, there was nothing but rubble of bricks and boards. Dear old WHS had fallen under the wrecking ball!

As I viewed the shambles, I thought, *Here, on this spot, is where I attended high school, where Wayne "bisected a given line segment," where Garland wrote in my autograph book, "Write me a letter as long as your arm," where the boys in the Model-A drove away, yelling to us girls, "Have a nice walk home!"*

Old Father Time has drawn his curtain on Winfield High. All that I have left are memories and an autograph book.❖

Dearest Ginny,
When twilight has drawn her curtain,
And pinned it with a star,
Remember that you have a friend,
No matter where you are.
And that's me,
Doris

Dear Ginny,
Two in a hammock,
Ready to kiss,
When all of sudden,
They went like this.
With love, Tiny

Dear Virginia,
Remember the days in Winfield school,
Remember the days in the old swimming pool,
Remember the good ole days in the ole school bus,
Remember me with just this verse.
Your classmate,
Charlotte.

Dear Virginia
Remember me early,
Remember me late,
Remember me as
Your classmate.
A true friend, Dotty

Dear Virginia,
Remember the day we slipped off from school and got some candy?
Virginia, the mail carrier!
Remember the day in Troy when we saw our boyfriends?
How did you like the basketball game when "our guys" (only they didn't know it!) played!
Always remember, "Them were the good ole days."
Your friend,
Mary.

Dear Virginia,
When the evening sun is setting,
When from care your mind is free,
When of others you are thinking, Will you sometimes think of me?
Your friend, J.T.

Virginia,
Always remember me as a friend in the sophomore class.
When you get married, and live on a farm,
Write me a letter as long as your arm.
A friend, Garland
P.S. Don't forget the first two weeks of your freshman year.

Bessie Mae Atkinson

By Dorothy Trebilcock

*L*ike many things of childhood, it seems so long ago, and then again, it's as though it was only yesterday. There was a little girl—me—in long, tan stockings and short bangs (the sides cut "just so the tips of the ears are showing," my mother used to say), and there was my friend. Bessie Mae Atkinson was her name. I can remember our first scrawlings on our kindergarten papers. She had to make her letters smaller than mine or she would run out of space, but she always painstakingly printed her full name: B-E-S-S-I-E M-A-E A-T-K-I-N-S-O-N.

Bessie Mae and I were very special friends, even though we were of different races. She was a pudgy sort of child with black hair drawn back from a dark face I shall never forget. A quick, impish smile lit her eyes and preceded the giggles that really were more than giggles. They shook her with high-pitched hilarity from head to toe, but mostly they stopped right in the middle. They weren't unkind guffaws; they were just happy, sometimes silly. In that small country school, I didn't learn the meaning of racism, discrimination or prejudice.

We traded apples and cookies. She always had a special gleam when she had "somethin' for you today!"

There were many good times Bessie Mae and I shared. Like the time we got out of step on the Highland Fling dance we were supposed to be learning. The austere Mrs. Brewster would step out in front of us, place her arched hand above her head and count, in tones that sounded like gongs of imminent doom: "One-two-three, left foot-right foot, left foot-right foot." And we would all hop obediently from foot to foot, bending our knees "just so." Bessie Mae and I got to laughing one day when class feet were waving in all the wrong directions. The exasperation of Mrs. Brewster was not concealed in her quiet, methodical counting.

"You and Bessie Mae may leave this room at once!" she shouted at me, and together we were banished to stand in the front hall. We didn't say much, but the twinkle never left Bessie Mae's eyes.

We were in the third grade when Bessie Mae's mother died. "My mama's gone," she told me. "She isn't ever coming back," she said, wiping a tear from her face with the edge of her puffed sleeve. Never in all time will I forget her reaching for her coat one cold, winter afternoon shortly afterward. She moved so slowly and sadly. I knew she was going home to a home without her mother. My heart ached then. It does still.

"Come home with me, Bessie Mae," I said. "My mother will fix us some cocoa and cookies." But she shook her head and trudged off alone.

Christmas was always the same in grade school in those days. There was a pageant, complete with the best sixth-grade reader solemnly intoning the words of Luke from atop a box richly camouflaged with large sheets of construction paper. As the story was told, the wise men and the shepherds all appeared walking slowly down an aisle bordered with parents craning expectant necks. Interspersed in the drama was each grade appearing as an "angel choir," singing an appropriate carol. A spotlight always shone on Mary as she sat holding the baby Jesus, a large doll borrowed from the kindergarten room. Mary usually sang a lullaby, and I remember the year I was selected for this honor. Bessie Mae always listened to me practice and once she smiled at me and said, "You sing pretty. It's kind of soft and quiet—like Mother Mary must have sung."

I remember that a dandy sore throat canceled my appearance the night of the program and I croakingly suggested that Bessie Mae take my place. She knew the song by heart, I knew, because she had sung it to me at recess while the other children were sliding on the icy pavement. She did take my place, and I asked my parents to go to the program.

"Bessie Mae sang the lullaby very well," my mother said.

"It was soft and quiet-like," my father added. I smiled through Musterole tears because I knew what he meant.

We traded apples and cookies. She always had a special gleam when she had "somethin' for you today!" Sometimes I had a few precious pennies, and together we would squander them in the depths of Mr. Earl's drugstore at the candy counter. Bessie Mae was the one who ran for towels the time I clunked my chin open on the second-floor steps, and she walked all the way to my house once when she found a mitten I had dropped on the playground.

When we were sixth graders, Bessie Mae and I were safety patroler. She reported her little brother, Nathaniel, one time because he had darted past the white flag. I can still hear the tongue-lashing he got, but every so often, she would stop and give him a big hug.

I remember so many things about Bessie Mae. I wonder where she is now and what she is doing. This was a time long before "minorities" and "power groups" and a preoccupation with identity as one or another. Perhaps it was the time and the place, or maybe it was the beautiful prerogative of childhood to accept unquestioningly what is good and honest and true, like friendship.

I remember Bessie Mae Atkinson, and I hope that sometimes she remembers me, too! ❖

Hand Pumps & Paper Cups

By Josie Patrick

At recess, we went to the hand pump at the back of the schoolhouse for a drink of water. The boys took turns pumping the water while the rest of us stood in line with the paper cups we'd made from our tablet or notebook paper. We folded the paper much as children nowadays fold it to make paper boats.

Those cups were pretty flimsy, but they were good for three or four swallows of water before they collapsed.

Sometimes, the pump emitted too big a gush and the cup fell apart before it could be jerked from under the stream. It all depended upon who was pumping. Those boys who pumped just right had to be masters of the art.

A few of the kids had tin cups that folded up to fit in the pocket. I graduated to one of those about the same time I graduated from union suits to bloomers and a fountain pen that I wore around my neck on a black velvet ribbon.

The water that sloshed over from the pump ran back into the well. Those standing closest got a foot washing. I strove to be as near the front of the line as possible. Some of those feet looked unpalatable.

Many times in the winter the pump was frozen stiff. Then the boys had to take a kettle of steaming water over to the pump where one worked the handle while the other poured the scalding water down the pipe to thaw out the ice.

Those same winter days were when one boy dared another to stick his tongue to the pump handle. If the dare was taken up, the pump wasn't the only thing needing a good unthawing!

There were days when the pump lost its prime. Then a couple of us girls were sent with a big bucket to the nearest neighbor's well. The boys might play hooky once they got off the school grounds.

The neighbor's well was beyond the back of the school yard, and we girls were permitted to travel over forbidden territory to reach it. Steps went up over the fence and down on the other side.

The girls' playground and outdoor rest room were on one side of the steps, while the boys' were on the other. It was an unbroken rule that we never crossed the boys' territory and that they never crossed ours, except on days when the pump lost its prime.

We two girls who were sent for the water let the bucket on the rope down into the well and put all our strength into pulling it up again. We trudged back to school with the brimming bucket sloshing its contents into our shoes.

The line of kids was already formed, all waiting to plunge their cups and hands into the bucket.

Somehow that water never tasted as good to me as did the water from the pump, unless I was far back in line at the pump and too many feet and shoes had been washed before I got up front with my cup. I didn't like the water from the bucket, even though I was often one of the girls who'd been allowed to walk forbidden territory to go fetch it. It might have been because Oscar Hill and Benny Fields, the two boys with the dirtiest hands in school, usually had their turn with their cups before me.❖

> *Many times in the winter the pump was frozen stiff. Then the boys had to pour the scalding water down the pipe to thaw out the ice.*

John Slobodnik

Two Against a Blizzard

By Carrol J. Carney

The wind was cold and the sky was dark that morning when my 9-year-old sister, Marie, and I started to school. I was 7. Our one-room schoolhouse was 2½ miles away. We had to walk, as did all the other kids in the neighborhood. We lived on a farm in the hill country of southwestern Missouri. Our older sisters and brothers had already quit school. In the early 1940s, it was the custom for kids to quit school just as soon as they were old enough to work around the farms. We had one brother not yet old enough to go to school.

Our road—if you could call it a road—was red clay. When it got wet, there was no going anywhere. The countryside along the road was littered with flint rocks and covered with scrub post oak and blackjack trees. They were bare of leaves except for a bunch of dead brown ones, now and then, that still clung to the limbs. Occasionally there was a cleared field, brown and dead, waiting for the onset of winter.

The teacher told the older kids to see that the smaller ones got home all right. But no one else walked our way.

We knew that if we didn't hurry we were going to get wet. The wind was rising and the clouds were getting darker. We alternately ran and walked, but it still caught us and we had to run the last part of the way to keep from being soaked. All morning the rain came down and the temperature dropped steadily. By midmorning, it was below freezing. The rain was changing to sleet and snow.

When noon came, the snow had already covered the ground and it was getting much colder. We had our lunch and stayed inside to play. We were all ganged up around the stove, trying to keep warm. The teacher told us that the storm should blow itself out before it was time to go home. This early in the season, the storms usually didn't last too long, nor were they too severe. But this one didn't let up. All afternoon the snow kept falling and the temperature continued to drop. The wind moaned and sang its cold song through the weather-beaten walls of the old school. Outside it piled the snow in drifts, some 2 feet high.

By the time to go home, the storm had worked itself into a full-blown blizzard. The teacher told the older kids to see that the smaller ones got home all right. But no one else walked our way. There was no reason to expect anyone to come from home; the only way they could get there would be to walk. Besides, this storm had caught everyone by surprise, and there would be all the livestock to care for. Out of necessity, that would have to be the first order of business for farmers.

We told our teacher that we would be all right and I was sure we would be. In fact, I was looking forward to getting out in the snow. Of course, I was dressed a little more warmly than Marie. In keeping with the times, she was wearing only a dress, as were just about all the other girls. We put on our coats and hats and started out.

We hadn't gotten out of the school yard and already we were out of sight. The snow swirled around us and the wind blew so hard that we could hardly make any headway. The first few minutes it was fun, running through the drifts. Soon though, the snow began to get in our shoes and melt, making our feet cold. We tried holding hands, but this, too, had to end; it was too cold. We had to put our hands in our pockets.

We hadn't gone very far when we began to realize what lay ahead of us. I was getting scared. We couldn't see very far in any direction, and the cold was getting to us fast. Marie was beginning to shiver and her teeth were chattering. But there was nothing to do but go on.

The drifts were piled high and the going was hard. Each time we came to a drift, I went through first to make a trail for her. Sometimes we couldn't see the drifts and we walked right into them. There was no sound except the wind. It howled and whipped the snow in our faces so badly that we could hardly see.

We pushed on. Our little world was just big enough so that we could see each side of the road; at least we wouldn't get lost. The cold seeped into our clothes and the wind made it feel like we were wearing nothing at all. This was especially true for Marie. The cold was sapping her strength fast. We had gone barely a mile when she began to slow down. After I broke through each drift, I would have to wait for her to catch up.

All the stories I'd ever heard of people being lost in blizzards were going through my mind.

In this world of freezing white, time seemed to stand still. It was as if we were moving in slow motion. Our legs were so tired that it was hard to put one foot in front of the other. My fear was heightened by the fact that my big sister was in worse shape than I was. The mind of a 7-year-old is very active under normal circumstances, and in this storm, mine was working overtime. All the stories I'd ever heard of people being lost in blizzards were going through my mind. I was sure there must be wild animals out there in the snow, just waiting for me to freeze so they could come and eat me. Maybe they wouldn't even wait for me to freeze.

I was scared, but I wasn't going to say anything to Marie. I would just stay close to her and we would get through. Thank goodness for the fence posts! At least we knew where we were going.

I knew, though, that the time would come when we would no longer have the fences. Our house was set at the far side of a large field, and we were going to have to cross that open field. Marie was stumbling a lot now, and I knew that she was cold almost beyond endurance. I held onto her arm as best I could and tried to help her along. Just ahead were the two large gateposts that told us it was time to turn into the field. From here on, it was all downhill. The entire field was a long, sloping hill and somewhere at the bottom was our house. In this storm, just to miss by a few feet meant that we would walk right by.

There was nothing to guide us now but our instincts. Marie was barely walking and I didn't think she really cared what happened; she was too cold. The wind had swept most of the snow off the hill. I thought this would make for easier walking, but I hadn't counted on the ice from the rain earlier in the day. The ground was so slick that we could hardly stand.

Among all my fears, there began to grow another very real fear, that of darkness. That time of year, dark came early on a clear day. That day it was going to come much earlier. We had no way of knowing how much time we had already spent. It seemed as if we had been out in this storm all our lives. I couldn't remember what it was like before we started out.

Marie slipped and fell on the ice. She cut her knees and they were bleeding. Each step she took, she would cry and then shiver. We were picking our way across the slick rocks when she fell down again; this time she didn't get up.

I went to her and asked her to get up before she froze. She just lay there, crying softly. I shook her. Then she told me to go on and leave her. She said she was too tired and sleepy to go on. If she could just sleep for a while, she'd be all right.

I wasn't very old, but I knew what would happen if she went to sleep. My fear was galvanized into real

John Slobodnik

panic. All the love and protective instinct that's in the heart of a 7-year-old brother came rushing to the surface. I grabbed her by the hands and tried dragging her across the frozen ground, all the time screaming at the top of my lungs, "You can't freeze out here, I won't let you freeze! If you don't come on, it's going to get dark and then we'll never get home! We'll get lost and some wild animals will get us!" Inch by inch, I dragged her across the ice.

I don't know whether it was the rough treatment or the fact that I managed to scare her out of her cold-induced sleep, but she did get up. With our arms around each other, we made our way on down the hill. The snow was deeper here; that meant that we were getting close to where we thought the house should be. *Oh! If we had missed it.* ... Just then, we saw the post of our yard fence ahead, and there, standing in the swirling snow, was the dim yet unmistakable outline of our old house. With newfound strength, we crossed the yard to the warm fire we knew would be waiting.

In the years that have followed that day long ago, I have had the good fortune to see many of the grand, majestic buildings of the world. None can compare to the memory we share of that old weather-beaten home, welcoming two small, half-frozen, exhausted, very scared school children.❖

Country School

By Edna Mae Busch

I was almost 10 when we moved from a small Iowa town to a farm on the prairies of central Minnesota. I remember my first days in a little, dilapidated country school that stood on one side of the big slough near a narrow, winding dirt road.

My older sister and I, wearing our best silk dresses, and my little brother made our way across the road and onto the playground during noon recess. Immediately we were the center of attention. My sister was fair skinned, with many freckles, and the big boys, almost full grown, set up a chant: "Freckles! Freckles!" The others took it up. We scurried into the old hall lined with hooks for coats, where syrup dinner pails sat in disarray on the floor.

We'd never been in a country school before. It was small, with the teacher's desk in front and the big, black heating stove in the opposite corner. How could it hold all 40 children? I soon found out, for I was first assigned to a big double seat. After that, I sat where anyone was missing, for attendance was very irregular.

The children filed in from recess. I thought of my bobbed hair as the girls passed by with long braids, dressed mostly in old-fashioned longer dresses and buttoned shoes with higher heels that had long since gone out of style. The pupils ranged in age from 5 years old to almost 20.

At recess, we picked the wildflowers from the prairie next to the school.

At recess, we picked the wildflowers from the prairie next to the school. Sometimes, on a dare from the boys, we would gingerly pick up the little garter snakes that slithered through the prairie grasses and whirl them around our heads. We helped carry water from the big slough and pour it into gopher holes while the boys waited with twine nooses to snare the striped gophers that came rushing out.

Once, one of the boys slipped two of the gophers into his pocket. He made a little harness, and while the teacher was busy writing on the blackboard, he "drove" them up and down the aisle.

We played ball with homemade balls and sticks for bats. Every evening we made new balls by wrapping rags around a stone, for they didn't last long. Finally, my older brother loaned us his bat. We always went home at noon, but no matter how fast we ate, the kids were always playing ball by the time we got back. One noon they informed me that they had already chosen up sides and I couldn't play. So after some argument, I got the bat and went to play on the other side of the schoolhouse with an older girl. Well, a real bat was better than a stick of wood, so after that I always got to play.

We also played a game—mumbletypeg—with pocketknives, balancing the point of the knife on the tip of our finger or thumb, the palm of the hand, the back of the wrist. Then, quickly, we'd flip the knife into the ground with a touch on the handle.

I developed my love for reading in that school. Every morning the teacher read to us from some good book.

The slough froze over in winter and became our playground. One of the teachers loaned me her old skates. Holding my coat open to catch the wind, I skimmed over the ice at breakneck speed, as if I had wings. But soon the teacher came outside with her little handbell and interrupted our fun. Sometimes, we pretended we didn't hear. Sometimes, some of the boys climbed up on the old coal shed and lay flat. Then, when the teacher came looking for them, they were nowhere in sight. We were always thirsty when we came in. We drank from cups made out of tablet paper. The water had been carried from the farm across the road.

The old heating stove almost cooked the pupils in the front desks, but those toward the back were stiff from cold. But that stove could put out a tremendous amount of heat, as one teacher found out. She

had put in a little more coal than usual. Later in the evening, when a strong wind came up, she began to worry. She persuaded her brother and his friend to check the school. It was hot inside—so hot that the thermometer had broken and the crayons had melted in the pupils' desks. Ringleaders in that school led the merciless teasing of a few selected victims. I didn't like it, but I didn't do anything to stop it, either. When the teacher brought her chubby little sister to school, these ringleaders said no one should play with her because she was fat. That time, I paid no attention. I played with her all day and we became instant friends.

I developed my love for reading in that school. Every morning the teacher read to us from some good book. I can remember hardly being able to wait until the next day to find out what happened in the next chapter. A huge bookcase filled with books stood behind my desk. I think I read every one of them—most of them when I should have been studying. I accomplished this by fitting the book inside my textbooks. When the teacher came down the aisle, I could conveniently shove the book into my desk.

It seemed every corner was always filled with some mischievous youngster with his face to the wall as punishment. The worst culprits were made to sit in the dark recess under the teacher's desk. Luckily, I never had to do that.

The first thing we did in the morning was march outside and stand in a circle around the flagpole while the flag was hoisted. Then we would all say the *Pledge of Allegiance*.

The old country school taught me many things. I had never learned phonics before, but I caught up there by watching and listening as the younger pupils learned "bat, mat, cat, fat, ring, wing, swing," etc. I learned my multiplication tables and addition that way also. I attended that school for three years and it still occupies an important niche in my memories. ❖

A Smelly Episode

By Kathryn V. King

It happened back in those days called "The Depression." I was a teacher in one of the rural schools of Kansas, although I was barely 18 years of age. I had completed a teacher's course during my four years of high school and passed a state teacher's examination, and so I was issued a certificate to teach.

On a cold January morning before classes began, I heard many excited voices just outside the schoolhouse. When I went out to investigate, I was informed that a skunk was under the building.

There was a hole in the foundation and, sure enough, when I edged close enough to see, I could see those familiar black and white stripes. There was no telltale odor as yet, so I shooed my students into the schoolhouse as fast as possible, hoping Mr. Skunk would leave peaceably and soon. My hopes were realized when we saw the skunk amble across the school yard and disappear into a nearby field.

The day proceeded as usual, although there was a lot of discussion about the unwanted visitor and whether he would return. Alice, one of my first-graders, declared that she was going to tell her brother, Jimmie, to catch the skunk in one of his traps. Jimmie often trapped wild animals for their pelts, which he sold.

From the sly grins on some of the older boys, I knew they were hoping the skunk would come back, and wondering what "Teacher" would do if he did. I made a vow to request that the hole in the foundation be closed up as soon as possible. I warned the children to stay away from the hole and play on the other side of the school yard.

The next morning, after classes had begun, I saw a boy pass by one of the windows. In a moment, I realized that he was Jimmie. I hurried to the door—just in time to hear a shot. All was still, and then bedlam broke loose as skunk fumes came through the floor of that old schoolhouse. Everyone dashed outside with streaming eyes, their lungs gasping for a breath of fresh air. Some became deathly ill from the sickening smell. Jimmie managed to drag a trap—with the dead skunk in it—out from under the building and left hurriedly, leaving me to cope with the situation. Opening the windows didn't help, so I started everyone home and I soon followed. Needless to say, none of us received a very warm welcome. Mothers especially were very irate—mine included.

Several methods were used to try to rid the building of the smell, including burning old rags and sulphur. Nothing helped much. Clothing was aired and cleaned, but the odor remained in those heavy winter clothes that we could not afford to discard. School resumed shortly, even though the smell was everywhere, even in book and supplies. How glad we all were when spring came and we could leave the door and windows open.

As for Jimmie—the son of one of the school-board members—he was more careful where he set his traps. ❖

> *There was no telltale odor as yet, so I shooed my students into the schoolhouse as fast as possible, hoping Mr. Skunk would leave peaceably and soon.*

Writing Wrongs

By Alan Sanderson

I always wanted to write, but I could never understand why so-called proper penmanship had to go along with it. Unfortunately for me, my teacher did, thereby presenting me with all sorts of problems during my school days, the biggest of which seemed to be the restricted use of my arm in making any kind of a line. I wrote (and still write) with a twitch of my fingers, as opposed to making graceful, circular swoops by moving my shoulder.

This, she said, was the reason my chalk squeaked while I tried to duplicate the numbers on the first-grade blackboard. When I explained that I didn't mind the occasional shrieks, she immediately informed me that *she* did. The sound set her teeth on edge.

Not wishing to have an edgy teacher, I replied at once that I'd try to do better. This wasn't easy, especially when she attempted to move my arm for me. As if this weren't enough, I had a devil of a time mastering the number 8. Those crisscrossed curves were just too much for me; that is, until I observed the boy standing next to me. He'd solved the difficulty by drawing two adjacent circles and tracing over their outlines to weld them together. It worked well for me, too—until my chalk began chirping again.

Once I was able to set down reasonable facsimiles of letters and figures, I was awarded a pencil. I thought my ordeals were a thing of the past—such were my fantastic hopes as I began my third year of schooling. Little did I know that pencils and the accompanying scraps of yellow paper were but a prelude to pens and white composition paper. I should have sensed something new was afoot the moment the duly authorized "ink monitor" was shown how to fill each inkwell resting in its hollow at the top right-hand corner of every pupil's desk. After that came the distribution of blotters, black wooden cylinders called penholders, and pen points.

Oh, those pen points were really something! Silver in color and about an inch long, they fitted snugly into a niche at the base of the penholder. A dip into the inkwell with one of those gadgets usually resulted in either too much fluid on the point, causing all kinds of frustrating blots, or too little to make a word or even a letter.

There were other hazards, such as my pen point snapping or splintering. Three points in a day, coupled with sighs and frowns from

Little did I know that pencils and the accompanying scraps of yellow paper were but a prelude to pens and white composition paper.

my teacher, were close to becoming a set rule. A bump from the desk in front or a jar from the one behind would add scribbles. I took a chance being stabbed by keeping this "weapon" inside my desk, for when I left my pen in the groove on top, it was frequently stolen.

Nevertheless, with these writing implements came a class period called "penmanship." It was conducted for 15 minutes in the morning, and I was harassed by it to the end of my elementary days. (Presumably, if a student hadn't learned to write clearly by then, he was no longer considered eligible to have his efforts underwritten by the town taxpayers.)

A notebook containing all the principles of *The Palmer Method* was presented to each student. In it were instructions for making our scratchings look something akin to their printed samples. The words didn't bother me too much. What did bother me were those interlocking circles and up-and-down patterns I was supposed to flawlessly recreate. Using the harsh, primitive tools at my disposal, my blot-adorned papers were rarely marked higher than "C." Scored in red, that was barely passing. In the beginning, I sought help during my lunch hour and after school. I had every desire to improve. Only when I was told that my troubles lay in not using my whole arm did I give up.

Upon graduation to high school and fountain pens, I found myself confronted by a different assortment of pitfalls. The freshmen group into which I'd been deposited was sternly advised on the very first day that no tests or homework done in pencil would be acceptable. Rather than accumulate a string of zeroes for my weekly report card, I took to keeping a pen in my pants pocket.

This was great until a hole developed in the lining from the other junk I carried about. A lost or forgotten fountain pen was only missed by its owner when test time loomed. It was quite a trick to maintain complete silence while finding someone in that class of 40 semi-alert

youngsters who had an extra pen to loan. Spelling out such dilemmas in frantic sign language attracted the wrong sort of person— like the teacher.

Coming equipped with two fountain pens— one clipped to the V-neck of my sweater and the other permanently cached in the heavy lining of my coat—seemed like an ideal solution. But one day my bright yellow pullover was spotted with inky designs. And soon afterward, I discovered a finger-staining wetness in the recesses of my mackinaw. Fill my slow-leak pens at school? No, that wasn't the answer. A bottle of ink was harder to locate than a fellow with a gross of pens, probably because, like me, everybody else was concerned about messy accidents in transit. Gosh, I couldn't even keep ink in a pen. How could I expect it to stay put in a bottle?

A bottle of ink was harder to locate than a fellow with a gross of pens, because, everybody was concerned about messy accidents.

Buying another one, not to mention a second spare, was too much of a drain on my weekly allowance. Making sure they were both wrapped in a handkerchief wasn't very practical when my mom had to wash them and my dad had to pay for them.

I was still pondering what to do when, miraculously, ballpoints burst upon the scene, shortly after the conclusion of the World War II. They appeared to be the antidote for all of my writing ills. Relatively cheap and not so apt to lose their ink, two of them found an immediate home among my school accessories. I had to be careful, however, not to lay my hand where I was about to scrawl with the newfangled things, since they wouldn't write over any amount of moisture. As a result, failure to hold my paper down sometimes produced stranger writing aberrations than the old pen points had.

Yet, I stuck with them. Eventually, I was rewarded with the improved models that would plow through anything. My words may not be "Palmer Method," or arm-swiveling perfect, but I can communicate with them, and isn't that all that's really necessary?❖

Little Boy's Troubles

I thought when I'd learned my letters
That all of my troubles were done;
But I find myself much mistaken—
They only have just begun.
Learning to read was awful,
But nothing like learning to write;
I'd be sorry to have to tell it,
But my copybook is a sight.

The ink gets over my fingers;
The pen cuts all sorts of shines,
And won't do all as I bid it,
The letters won't stay on the lines,
But go up and down and all over,
As though they were dancing a jig—
They are there in all shapes and sizes,
Medium, little and big.

The tails of the Y's are so contrary;
The handles get on
the wrong side
Of the D's and the K's
and the H's,
Though I've certainly
tried and tried.

To make them just right,
it is dreadful.
I really don't know what to do;
I'm getting almost distracted—
My teacher says she is, too.

There'd be so much comfort
in learning,
If one should get through; instead
Of that, there are books awaiting,
Quite enough to craze my head,
And grammar—Oh dear me,
There's no good place for stopping,
When one has begun, I see.
My teacher says little by little,
To the mountaintop we climb.
It isn't all done in a minute,
But only a step at a time.
She says that all the wise
and learned men
Has each to begin as I do.
If that's so—where's my pen?

—Charlotte Perry

Blackmail

By Helen Johnson

Anyone who lived in a small town around 1908 knew what "marble season" was all about.

That year, I was in the third grade of the Redfield, S.D., grammar school. It was springtime and the young men's fancies turned to thoughts of marbles. They played in their yards, on the streets, anywhere that youngsters congregated.

At school, too, the boys' minds were on marbles. My brother, Fred, was one of Redfield's undisputed champions of the game, and my school days were made quite miserable for awhile by someone who was after my brother's prize marbles.

He was a boy named Jonas, and unfortunately he sat behind me. I thought he was hateful since he teased and tormented me endlessly. His appearance bothered me, too; he was larger and meaner-looking than the other boys and already wore long pants, which made him seem older than his friends.

"If you don't give me two of your brother's marbles, I'm gonna sit with you tomorrow."

Some children shared their desks, often with their sisters or brothers, but I had a large desk all to myself. Jonas sat right behind me, breathing down my neck and threatening to come up and sit with me. He scared me half to death, especially when he pretended that he was about to slide into my desk seat. I nearly fell out of my seat when he tried that one.

One day, Jonas grumbled an ultimatum: "If you don't give me two of your brother's marbles, I'm gonna sit with you tomorrow."

That threat was sufficiently scary to send me scampering into Fred's room after school, searching for his bagful of beautiful marbles. With much nervousness, I pocketed two of the beauties and presented them to Jonas the next morning.

Of course, once Jonas saw how easy it was to scare and threaten me, he kept it up. Every day I was instructed to bring another marble or two from my brother's collection.

Finally, Fred realized that his precious marble supply was dwindling rapidly, and he hid the bag. He hid it so well that my frantic search for his marbles was fruitless. I dreaded showing up at school the next day empty-handed, but show up I did. Jonas was true to his word. But as he crept forward to take over half of my seat, I shrieked nervously and fell to the floor!

Our teacher, a nice young lady and a friend of my older sisters, sprang to my rescue. "So you like to sit with girls," she said to my tormentor. "Well, I will just let you do that."

She had him move around to all the girls' desks, sharing their seats for awhile, and when two girls were already sharing a desk, the teacher had Jonas sit between them. His face was flaming with embarrassment and shame. The classroom was in an uproar, and I was in tears from fear and humiliation.

After the commotion had died down, the teacher tried to comfort me. She even walked home with me after school. I was shy and very much in awe of her, and thrilled that she was my sisters' friend.

I told her all about taking Fred's marbles to give to Jonas, and she saw to it that my brother's precious collection was returned to him. But the greatest thing was the way Jonas treated me after the incident: He never spoke to me again!❖

Ladies Don't Fight

By Julia Rankin

It was my first year at the little one-room log schoolhouse. I was 6 years old.

At the little recess on a winter morning, I was playing crack the whip with other little girls when I noticed Guy McFee watching us. He had a silly grin on his ugly face, and I knew he was thinking up something mean to do—he always did. He was about my age, but bigger. When I came by him in the game, he stuck out his foot and tripped me. Down I went onto the hard gravel, skinning my knee.

It really hurt and I was hopping mad. I picked up a jagged rock and threw it at him. Usually I can't hit anything I throw at, but that time, I hit him smack on the nose. He yelled and grabbed his nose, which was bleeding something awful—blood all down the front of his shirt.

The teacher came running. She saw it was a bad nosebleed, so she sent a big girl to get a bundle of rags from her desk, and led Guy to the water bench. She soaked clean rags in cold water and told Guy to hold them on his nose.

The teacher took mutton tallow from her emergency supplies and warmed it at the wood-burning stove until it was soft, then applied it to his injured nose. In the meantime, I was peeping from behind the curious children. I was scared and my knee hurt.

The teacher learned that I was mixed up in the "accident" and tried to find out what had happened, but Guy accused me, and I accused him. Exasperated, she sent him home to have his mother patch his nose and give him a clean shirt.

Then the teacher noticed my bleeding knee and my dirty, tear-streaked face. Wearily, she reached for the bandages and mutton tallow again. She doctored my knee and washed my face, then looked at me and sighed, "You're too little to go home by yourself. I'd be in trouble with your mother and father if I sent you. That knee will be stiff by the end of school, but it can't be helped."

She sighed again and rang the bell. The little recess that had turned into a big recess was ended and we began school again.

"I hope all of you know your lessons today," the worried teacher said. "We'll have to cut classes short to keep to our usual schedule."

My knee did get stiff, and it hurt, but I hobbled home with the usual group of children who lived out my way. When I got there, Mama asked how I'd hurt my knee while she soaked dried sassafras leaves for a poultice and tied it on.

I told her I'd fallen while playing crack the whip with the other girls. Well, that was true— as far as it went. After Sunday school the next Sunday, Papa noticed Guy's scratched, bruised nose. "Guy, you've been fighting," he said in a scolding voice.

I hid behind Papa and peeped around at Guy. I was scared and expected him to tell Papa that I had hit him with a rock, but Guy just squirmed guiltily, so Papa went on with his lecture: "My girls are not always as good as they should be, but they don't fight."

But Guy didn't even look up; he just rubbed his toe in the ground. Guy was a gentleman. He didn't tell on a lady.❖

A Fall From Grace

By Norman M. Cheney

We returned to school after our summer vacation on Sept. 6. A few days later, a huge wagonload of firewood was delivered and dumped near the back door. It was wood for our Acme box stove, which heated our schoolroom in the winter.

Teacher came out and inspected the wood. She gave her approval and signed the bill.

After the team had left, she said to me, "Norman, I would like to have you and a couple of other boys work after school and pile the wood against the wall in the back hall." She continued, "I will pay each of you 50 cents."

I accepted and ran to tell Bill. He was playing marbles with his friend, Paul Meurisse. They agreed to help me.

After school, we ran home and told Mother. She gave us her consent, with a warning: "You be sure you come home in time to milk and do the chores."

The following afternoon, when school let out, we were ready for work. Teacher brought out a 6-foot wooden stepladder from a broom closet.

We worked in brigade style, Bill and Paul handing the wood along to me, and I stacked it. We worked steadily and the pile grew higher and higher.

We were working on the second row when I noticed a trapdoor in the ceiling. As with Pandora's box, curiosity drove me to find out what was in the attic.

I climbed the ladder, and standing on the top step, I could reach the trapdoor. Yelling to my helpers, I pushed the door open and peered into the dark interior. The only light came from tiny ventilating windows on each side of the building.

There was no floor. I could see the laths on the ceiling between the joists that ran the length of the attic. The boys joined me, and I warned them not to step on the ceiling; it would not hold their weight.

They waited for me to lead the way. I stepped boldly along the joists for 10 feet. Then I lost my balance and stepped on the ceiling, which promptly broke. I fell through the hole, down into the schoolroom 10 feet below.

Teacher, who was working on papers at her desk, screamed as I landed on the stove, which tipped over, ripping the funnel down and covering me with soot.

She came running over to me and helped me up, asking, "What in the world were you doing in the attic?"

I felt a bump on the side of my head and winced. She brought a cloth dipped in cold water and washed my face. I thanked her as I limped to the door. Bill was waiting outside, his face white with fear. We walked slowly home.

When Mother saw me, she sighed and said, "I might have known you would get into trouble." She added, with a twinkle in her eyes, "Were you imitating Al Jolson or making up for a minstrel show?"

I was hurting too much for much laughter, but I sure thought her remarks were amusing later when I had cooled.

Meanwhile, Bill had taken care of the chores. He brought the milk in and placed the pail on the sink shelf. He looked at me and broke out laughing. He said, "Brother, you sure messed things up."

I had no answer. Mother washed my face in warm water and patted Vaseline on the bump. When she was finished, she said, "You had no business climbing into the attic. I am sure your father will not appreciate paying the repair bill."

Mother was right, as usual. Father cut off my allowance for three months.

I also learned a lesson. Fools rush in where angels fear to tread. ❖

Spring Fishing

By Eugene P. Kernutt

was born in 1900 in Harrisonville, Ill., in Monroe County. My parents moved to Missouri when I was 1 year old. The town at that time was called Maplewood; it is in St. Louis County. I lived in Maplewood for 40 years.

I started going to school in Maplewood at 6 years of age. I finished school when I was 15 years old.

When we were dismissed from school for vacation, we used to sing a special song on our way home from school: "No more pencils, no more books, no more teacher's cross-eyed looks."

When I was 9 years old, I was no angel. My teacher, Miss Ella Smith, was 84 years old, and boy, was she strict. I can't brag about it; I stayed in her room two terms.

One beautiful spring day, I sat daydreaming out the window, watching anglers heading toward a nearby stream to fish. I couldn't see myself sitting in school another day, so I played hooky on the morrow and went fishing.

I couldn't see myself sitting in school another day, so I played hooky on the morrow and went fishing.

When I was a boy, I always carried a pocketknife and a fishing line in my pocket. When I got to the creek, I cut me a fishing pole and dug a few worms.

I don't remember just how many I caught, but it was six or seven bullheads, 8 inches long. Boy, now I was up a tree. If I took them home, I would get a licking for skipping school. But I didn't want to throw them back.

I saw a man walking down by the creek, and asked him if he wanted to buy my fish. He asked how much I wanted. I told him a dime, and he took the fish.

Then he smiled and asked why I wasn't in school. It turned out he was the district's truant officer. I have to admit that I got that licking anyway!❖

The nursery rhyme *Mary's Lamb* is a little ditty that many of us back in the Good Old Days learned first as a poem and then as a song. It was one of the first melodies many piano students learned to plunk out on an old upright.

The words and illustration reprinted here came from *Nurseryland Jingles*, a small volume of rhymes published in 1915 by Gabriel Sons & Co. of New York.

Mary's Lamb

Mary had a little lamb,
    Its fleece was white as snow;
And everywhere that Mary went
    The lamb was sure to go.

He followed her to school one day,
    Which was against the rule;
It made the children laugh and play
    To see a lamb at school.

And so the teacher turned him out,
    But still he lingered near,
And waited patiently about
    Till Mary did appear.

Then he ran to her, and laid
    His head upon her arms,
As if he said, "I'm not afraid,—
    You'll keep me from all harm."

"What makes the lamb love Mary so?"
    The eager children cry.
"Oh, Mary loves the lamb, you know,"
    The teacher did reply.

And you each gentle animal
    In confidence may bind,
And make it follow at your will,
    If you are only kind.